Livwise

easy recipes for a healthy, happy life

Olivia Newton-John

LYONS PRESS
Guilford, Connecticut
An imprint of Globe Pequot Press

Metric Conversion Tables

Approximate U.S. Metric Equivalents

Liquid Ingredients

U.S. MEASURES	METRIC	U.S. MEASURES	METRIC
¼ TSP.	1.23 ML	2 TBSP.	29.57 ML
½ TSP.	2.36 ML	3 TBSP.	44.36 ML
¾ TSP.	3.70 ML	¼ CUP	59.15 ML
1 TSP.	4.93 ML	½ CUP	118.30 ML
1¼ TSP.	6.16 ML	1 CUP	236.59 ML
1½ TSP.	7.39 ML	2 CUPS OR 1 PT.	473.18 ML
1¾ TSP.	8.63 ML	3 CUPS	709.77 ML
2 TSP.	9.86 ML	4 CUPS OR 1 QT.	946.36 ML
1 TBSP.	14.79 ML	4 QTS. OR 1 GAL.	3.79 LT

Dry Ingredients

U.S. MEASURES		METRIC	U.S. MEASURES	METRIC
17⅗ OZ.	1 LIVRE	500 G	2 OZ.	60 (56.6) G
16 OZ.	1 LB.	454 G	1¾ OZ.	50 G
8⅞ OZ.		250 G	1 OZ.	30 (28.3) G
5¼ OZ.		150 G	⅞ OZ.	25 G
4½ OZ.		125 G	¾ OZ.	21 (21.3) G
4 OZ.		115 (113.2) G	½ OZ.	15 (14.2) G
3½ OZ.		100 G	¼ OZ.	7 (7.1) G
3 OZ.		85 (84.9) G	⅛ OZ.	3½ (3.5) G
2⅘ OZ.		80 G	¹⁄₁₆ OZ.	2 (1.8) G

Contents

introduction

This is my first book — ever! Who would have thought it would be a cookbook? Over my lifetime I have made two attempts at writing a book but didn't finish either of them. This book means more to me than my previous attempts as it isn't about my personal life, but my life experience with food, the effect it has on my body and how eating the right foods in combination has helped to keep me fit and healthy.

There is an old, familiar saying "We are what we eat!" and I am a firm believer that what we put into our bodies creates the building blocks of our existence. I also believe that what we think about what we eat is just as important. Considering where food is grown, how it is transported and stored, and finally, how it is prepared, means that each meal can be gratefully received and enjoyed as the precious gift that it is. Every plant and animal once had life, and each time I eat, I try to acknowledge this and honor that life with a quiet grace.

There are thousands of cookbooks on the market but what makes this one so special is not just my own passion for the role food has in maintaining good health, but the support I have had in compiling the recipes. I have been fortunate to be able to include recipes written by some of my favorite people, whose taste buds I respect. The contributors in this book have not only devoted their time, but also their knowledge of food and experience in the kitchen to ensure that this collection of recipes not only reflects the way I like to eat, but may help set you on the path to a healthier lifestyle.

Naturally, my first port of call was to all the talented chefs, both past and present, at Gaia Retreat and Spa in Byron Bay, Australia (www.gaiaretreat.com.au) — which in my opinion is the best healing retreat in the world, and my favorite place to eat. As co-owner, I was proud to develop an organic garden at the retreat so that the food we serve can be picked fresh each day — just a part of what makes mealtimes at Gaia so special.

Karen Inge, a well-respected nutritionist from Melbourne, Australia, was also asked to contribute to *LivWise*. I have been lucky enough to dine at Karen's table and her food is always delicious, nutritious and beautiful to behold!

In early 2010 I was in Australia fundraising for The Olivia Newton-John Cancer and Wellness Centre (ONJCWC) and someone gave me a book to read called *From Cancer to Wellness: The Forgotten Secrets*. I couldn't put it down. It was written by Kristine Matheson, also a cancer thriver, who, as coincidence would have it, lives very close to Gaia Retreat. I was so impressed with her book and her thoughts on raw food that I immediately asked if she would contribute some of her recipes and she kindly has.

The common thread between all these recipes is the food philosophy behind them and a mutual respect for the importance of eating a healthy balanced diet and increasing your intake of plant foods, some raw as well as organic foods where possible. Along with regular exercise, this helps your body find its own natural balance and achieve a healthy weight. The aim of this book therefore is to introduce you to ways of eating that will help to keep you in good health, whether you are going through the cancer journey or just wanting to maintain optimum health.

We have included many tasty simple vegetarian meals within these covers. You can add fish or meat as you wish, but I'm always pleasantly surprised at how satisfying vegetarian meals can be on their own. We all agree that you have to enjoy what you eat, so there are also sweet treats included.

I am very proud to say that 100 percent of the profits I receive from the sale of *LivWise* will support the Olivia Newton-John Cancer and Wellness Centre (www.oliviaappeal.com) to help make available cutting-edge treatments and support cancer research. I am proud to say it will include a dedicated Wellness Centre with complementary programs, such as massage, yoga and music therapy and so much more, that focus on the needs of the whole person — body, mind and spirit. It is a center I dreamed of as I was going through my cancer journey. Ultimately, my vision is that cancer will become a footnote in history.

Love and light,
Olivia

the common sense diet

Now that I am eighteen years past my initial diagnosis of breast cancer and feeling better than I've ever felt before I think of myself as a cancer thriver! People often ask me what my secret is and want to know how I manage to stay slim, active and healthy at my age — I feel timeless and even though my passport says so it is hard for me to comprehend that I am 62 years young!

I am no cordon bleu chef, nor am I a doctor or nutritionist, but I have picked up some pieces of information over the years about health and nutrition. Without getting too complicated, I wanted to present in this book some of what I do to stay healthy.

As I sat down to write this book I began to realize how many different eating choices I have succumbed to over the years. I have been a vegetarian at times, followed a strict macrobiotic diet on occasion, restricted my dairy and wheat intake on and off and have now returned to a more balanced diet that includes chicken and fish and occasionally some red meat. I am a very simple cook and like to keep things pretty basic in the kitchen (thanks Mum!). I believe first and foremost that simplicity is the key to healthy eating. I love eating this way as I can taste the freshness of my food. To me it seems obvious — when I start adding heavy sauces and toppings to meals I get into trouble!

The simplest way for me to explain my food philosophy is to remember that what goes up must come down. What you eat goes in, and if it doesn't come out it has to go somewhere else — like on your hips! I believe it starts with a combination of controlling the portion size of what goes in, ensuring the food is of the best quality you can find (organic is preferable), exercising regularly, drinking lots of water, and eating enough fiber to keep your internal wheels turning so you can expel the waste, and any toxins, efficiently.

Of course, following a diet can be hard to do over long periods of time. I am lucky I have a quick metabolism and I listen to my body. If I eat a large amount of food one day, the next day my body will tell me to ease up. I cut back on my food intake and do a workout. That way, I never let my body accrue extra pounds.

From what I have learned over the years the one thing that everybody seems to agree upon is that combining a balanced diet with regular exercise and clean water (and, I believe, a positive attitude) is the best-known way to stay healthy. A balanced diet should consist mostly of plants, vegetables and fruit, some whole grains, nuts and seeds. It should include some protein-rich foods such as fish, poultry, eggs, dairy, legumes (beans and lentils) and a small amount of healthy fats, such as avocados, nuts, seeds and seed oils, olive oil and oily fish.

This is basically the eating regime I follow. It's not really a secret at all. I call it the common sense diet!

listen to your instincts

In all areas of my life I have learned to trust my instincts — after all, they once saved my life. After finding a lump in my breast (it wasn't the first, but all the others had been benign) I went to the doctor to have it checked. I was sent for a mammogram, which was negative. I then had a needle biopsy, which also turned out to be negative. I still wasn't feeling right in myself or with the lump, which was a little tender, so my doctor and I decided I should undergo some exploratory surgery. Although I had heard that breast cancer wasn't necessarily tender to the touch, this was my experience, and I'm glad I listened to my instincts and persevered.

In the end they found that the lump in my breast was cancerous. The cancer was removed, I had reconstructive surgery and underwent chemotherapy for about eight months. I have yearly mammograms now, and although the medical term used is "remission," I don't like that word; it sounds like the cancer is lurking — I say it's gone! I tell this story not to scare women but to encourage them to do regular self-breast examinations and to trust themselves and their instincts if they feel something isn't right. (For more detailed information about how to do this yourself you can download a copy of a step-by-step breast self exam on my website www.liv.com.)

This experience reinforced the general idea that listening to your body and being conscious of the role nutrition can play in decreasing the risk of disease and helping to restore your body to its natural state of balance is so important.

After my experience with breast cancer I became even more conscious of what I was eating and tried the macrobiotic diet of Michio Kushi, one of the early leaders of the macrobiotic movement. I had heard that a macrobiotic diet was very cleansing

and gave the body a chance to heal itself. In a nutshell, macrobiotics is all about eating food that is as natural as possible and avoiding foods that have been highly processed and refined. At the time I was eating a low-fat, high-fiber diet that did not include any meat, dairy products or sugar. A macrobiotic diet typically consists of about 60 percent whole grains, 30 percent vegetables (it encourages you to eat these raw where possible) and the remaining 10 percent is made up of bean and bean products, such as tempeh and tofu. It encourages people to eat some fruits and consume nuts and seeds in moderation while at the same time places emphasis on eating food grown locally and in season.

When I was going through treatment I employed a chef for a few months to cook my macrobiotic meals. I eventually eased my way out of the rigidity of the diet but learned to respect much of its philosophy.

Luckily my mother, Irene, who was born and raised in Germany, set great food examples for me when I was a child. She fed me healthy food — rye and pumpernickel bread instead of white bread sandwiches in my lunchbox and dinners that almost always consisted of steamed potatoes (skins included), steamed broccoli and carrots. We ate plenty of fresh salads, delicious dishes of red cabbage made the German way with apples, and steamed or baked chicken breast or fish. For dessert we would have baked apples, pears or whatever fruit was in season, topped with a dollop of yogurt. Mum would often make her own yogurt, and always insisted that it was terrific for our digestive systems and she was right — probiotic yogurt (the kind that contains health-promoting live bacteria) is still a favorite of mine.

It was all very simple and basic cooking, and while I was annoyed at the time that I wasn't able

to have the deep-fried snacks and cakes my friends enjoyed after school, I now thank her for those early years of eating training that have made such a huge difference throughout my adult life. This doesn't mean I don't enjoy sweets like the next person. I have a very sweet tooth which I also attribute to my mother. When she passed away we found chocolate hidden in just about every cupboard! Luckily for me, there have been research studies that show that chocolate can assist blood flow to the brain and is rumored to release a chemical endorphin that makes you feel like you're in love, so it can't be all bad. I think my mother must have known this instinctively, without research!

From experimenting with many various diets over the years I have learned that it is important to listen to your body. We all have instincts and I pay close attention to mine in relation to food and the way it affects me.

LivWise organically

I always look for, and try to buy, organically. Organic food contains fewer pesticides and toxins. It is my belief that eating organically as much as possible really does make a difference to our overall health.

There are countless pesticides used in the cultivation of mass-produced fruit and vegetables, most of which have never been tested on humans. This is an issue that I became very involved with when my dear friends, Nancy and Jim Chuda, lost their five-year-old daughter, Colette, to Wilms Tumor — a kidney cancer that is believed to be environmentally caused. She was my daughter Chloe's best friend and it was a heartbreaking experience for us all. The Chudas' incredible spirit and their strong Buddhist faith helped them create something positive out of their pain, an organization called Healthy Child Healthy World (www.healthychild.org) to inform parents of the toxins that their children are exposed to in their everyday environment, including the chemicals found in food. I am proud to say that the organization is now aligned with webmd.com, the most respected online source of medical information in the world.

Buying organically supports the organic produce industry and our spending dollars can effect change and increase the demand for organically grown food. I also try to buy locally grown — it is bound to be fresher, taste better, and saves the fossil-fuel costs of storage and transportation. Most importantly though, seeking out organic produce means you are not ingesting the pesticides that are still allowed to contaminate some of our foods and products.

As I like to limit my exposure to chemicals as much as I possibly can — at least to the ones I know about — I am pleased to see that most supermarkets are now carrying a variety of organic foods, fruits and vegetables.

anti what?

It has taken a few years of trial and error to find the diet that suits my body best, but the recipes in this cookbook represent the kinds of foods I now love to eat (some cooked and some raw), and they are tasty, healthy and delicious too!

I have done a lot of reading about diets and words like "antioxidant" keep cropping up. "Antioxidant" is a word I see everywhere. For a while I never really understood what it meant, but was too embarrassed to admit it!

I remember from school that oxidation means basically, to rust, and that "anti" means "against" but in order to understand the role of antioxidants you need to understand what these agents are opposing. In much the same way as oxidation creates rust, causing a breakdown on the surface of inanimate objects, oxidation inside the body causes a breakdown of the cells. The particles produced by this breakdown are called free radicals and they attack healthy cells. This chain of events weakens your immune functions and speeds up aging and studies show links to various forms of diseases, such as cancer, heart disease and many other degenerative conditions.

When you cut an apple or an avocado and squeeze lemon over the fruit, it will not go brown — or oxidize — but rather stay its original color as you are preventing the process of oxidation, or at least slowing it down. The vitamin C, an antioxidant vitamin in the lemon, is doing it right in front of your eyes.

Ideally, we want to get rid of those "radicals" and one way of doing this is to eat properly, avoid stress and cut back on the habits that promote them, such as smoking, drinking, eating poorly and the one we can't always avoid, pollution from the environment.

In basic terms, vegetables and fruits with the strongest colors are generally rich with antioxidants and high in vitamins and minerals. Oranges, red peppers, tomatoes, spinach and carrots are all good examples of foods rich in these nutrients, to name a few. Culinary herbs and spices are also wonderful sources of powerful antioxidants and even when you add just a handful of fresh herbs to a salad you increase the antioxidant capacity of that salad by 200 percent.

the good, the bad and the spooky

Every time I go to the doctor she checks my cholesterol levels — and for good reason. I know that smoking (luckily I don't smoke) and consuming foods high in fat (bad fat anyway) can push your cholesterol over the top. Interestingly, cholesterol only comes from animals and animal products — never from plants — so a diet rich in

vegetables and fruits is looking better and better as I get older!

Although most of us think of it as a bad thing, cholesterol has a number of important functions in the body including the production of hormones, vitamin D and bile acids. A waxy substance, the majority of cholesterol in the body is made in the liver from saturated fats and the remainder comes from cholesterol in food.

Because cholesterol is a fatty substance, it doesn't dissolve in the bloodstream and needs to be transported around the body on a protein carrier called lipoprotein. The two major carriers of cholesterol are high-density lipoproteins (HDL), also know as "good" cholesterol because they tend to take the cholesterol away from the arteries, back to the liver, and low-density lipoproteins (LDL), known as "bad" cholesterol. I have come up with my own acronym to explain these: Happy and Delightful for the good fats and Lazy and Disgusting, for the fats we don't want!

It worries me when people try to take fats completely out of their diets to lose weight because we need some fats in our body to produce hormones and repair our cell membranes and for the creation of vitamin D, for healthy bones and teeth. But if there is an excess of the LDL (the lazy bad dude) in our body, it ends up sticking to our arteries and causing all kinds of problems — they call it plaque. When this plaque builds up in the arteries of the heart and brain it can cause strokes and heart attacks.

The spooky part is that there are not necessarily any symptoms. This is why a healthy diet and exercise are so important. We need to keep the blood pumping to exercise the heart muscle, ensure our arteries are elastic, and keep an eye on our Happy and Lazy ratio.

The aim is to try and eat less saturated and

trans fats (both of which increase LDL cholesterol) and replace them with healthy fats, such as monounsaturated and polyunsaturated fats.

Over-consuming foods with saturated fats and trans fats in them can increase the risk of heart disease. These include foods like whole milk, cheese, butter and fatty meat products. Trans fats are unhealthy substances that are formed when oils are solidified during a chemical process called hydrogenation. Trans fats can also be found in things like take-out meals, packaged snacks, commercially packaged baked items such as crackers, biscuits, doughnuts, muffins, cakes, pies and processed meat products. These are all examples of foods that can contain fats that are not good for you. I admit that I do eat some of these foods (I'm human after all!) but in moderation — that is the key.

So what about the good fats? In general, monounsaturated and polyunsaturated fats can help lower blood cholesterol levels. Foods high in these fats include most nuts and seeds and a variety of vegetable oils. The two types of polyunsaturated fats that affect our health most positively are omega-3 and omega-6. According to the Australian Heart Foundation these can be found in oily fish, such as tuna, salmon, sardines and blue mackerel along with things like tahini, flaxseeds, sunflower and safflower oil, pine nuts, walnuts and Brazil nuts.

I believe the most important of all these happy fats is omega-3. If you can't get it from fresh fish it can be obtained from good-quality fish oil supplements, flaxseed oil or oil derived from algae. As well as aiding with heart health by lowering blood pressure, blood fats and reducing the stickiness of platelets, omega-3s are also crucial for brain development and cognitive function and evidence has shown them to have anti-inflammatory effects. We should be trying to eat oily fish at least twice a week. All this and I find it also helps improve my hair and skin, too!

water, water all around and not a drop to drink

Wonderful refreshing and delicious, bubbly or flat, mineralized or distilled, pH balanced and alkaline — so many kinds of water!

I always love going to Australia, but especially because you can still fill a kettle for your cup of tea with tap water. These days, in many parts of the world, it is considered a rarity to be able to do this.

It is commonly believed that between 60 and 70 percent of our body is made up of water. The jury is out on exactly how much water we should consume daily, but it seems logical that we should at least replace what we lose every day in perspiration, elimination and breathing!

According to the Mayo Clinic, we lose an average of about 6 cups of fluid a day through perspiration and breathing, and another 4 cups for elimination. By that math, we need to drink at least 10 cups of water to make up for all our bodily functions and help cleanse our system of toxins. I try to drink at least 6–8 cups of water a day, including a coffee and a few cups of tea. Foods with a high water content, like most fruit and vegetables, can also count toward our fluid intake.

I notice throughout the day that I become very tired when I am dehydrated. I find that I will experience an afternoon lull when I have forgotten to drink water — and it often mimics hunger — an unfortunate mimic because it leads to snacking on all kinds of yummy bad food!

taking your pulses!

Our bodies need protein to repair cells. Meats and fish are probably the most well-known sources of protein, but protein can also be obtained from plants although most plant foods except soy do not supply all of the amino acids and so are often referred to as incomplete proteins. Good plant sources include a variety of legumes (in Australia, dried legumes are known as pulses) such as lentils and chickpeas; a variety of beans including red kidney, lima, pinto, black, white, butter, borlotti, cannellini, navy and adzuki beans; as well as split peas, nuts and seeds. Ideally, these should be combined with grains such as rice to make a "complete protein." Fermented soy products such as tempeh, miso and tofu are all complete proteins. Protein can also be found in some vegetables, including mushrooms, coconut, corn, peas, spirulina, algae and barley greens.

Eggs are also an excellent source of protein and choline, plus an array of minerals and other nutrients. We love them in our house and eat them almost every day!

It is true that eggs contain cholesterol but dietary cholesterol has very little bearing on blood cholesterol and it is generally believed that if you cut back on saturated and trans fats you should still be able to eat one egg a day without raising your cholesterol. I try to look for organic free-range eggs where the hens have been raised with freedom and without hormones and antibiotics. Happy hens make better eggs!

the green, green grass of home

Every health book I've read sings the praises and stresses the importance of green food and drinks in our diet. Near our home in Florida is an amazing place called the Hippocrates Health Institute. They are famous for their natural health care and were the first to introduce me to the value of wheatgrass. They grow it on the premises and juice it fresh several times daily. Within only a couple of days of drinking this nutritious, cleansing and "living" drink I felt wonderfully alive and vital. The woman who founded Hippocrates, Ann Wigmore, claimed to have cured herself of cancer by eating "live" foods (www.hippocratesinst.org). It's amazing to think that some of the world's largest and strongest creatures survive on grass alone. Not that I recommend that for us!

Sprouts are a living food that release and supply energy to all the cells in the body. They have anti-aging benefits and are recognized for their high level of enzyme activity. The most essential enzymes in sprouts are amylase, protease and lipase, which are all extremely helpful in aiding digestion.

sprouting can be fun

Good-quality sprouts are often available at health food stores, but you can also grow them yourself. The following seeds, grains and legumes can be sprouted. Only use organic seeds, legumes, grains and nuts for sprouting. Non-organic produce contains chemicals and may not sprout.

Seeds: alfalfa, broccoli, celery, clover, oats, radish, fenugreek, pumpkin seeds, sunflower seeds.

Grains: buckwheat, barley, millet, rice, wheat.

Legumes: chickpeas, lentils, mung beans and soybeans.

Nuts: almonds, cashews, walnuts, pecans, pistachios.

Anyone, anywhere can create their own sprouts. All you need is the right equipment. You can either buy a ready-made kit that includes seeds, or alternatively you can create your own using 8 cup capacity glass jars with a wide mouth. If you are using your own equipment you will also need a square of cheesecloth that can be cut to size and used for lids, as well as a few rubber bands to fix the lid to the jar.

how to sprout

Place 2–4 tablespoons of any of the seeds or grains listed above in a jar — do not mix varieties as they will reach maturity at different times.

Pour in enough filtered pure water to half-fill the jar. Place the cheesecloth over the top and seal with a rubber band. Leave to soak for at least 6 hours. Drain the seeds, rinse well and turn the jar upside down to drain completely — this prevents rotting.

Rinse with pure filtered water twice a day.

Germination will take place and the seeds and grains will expand by about eight times their original size (keep this in mind when adding them to the jar).

Legumes and nuts will not expand at the same rate as seeds and grains. Place 1 cup of legumes or nuts in a jar as above and fill with filtered pure water. Set aside at room temperature to soak for at least 15 hours. Continue to wash and drain the legumes and nuts twice a day, even after germination begins, until they are ready to eat. See the chart below for more details.

sweets for my sweet, sugar for my honey

As I said, I have a very sweet tooth but I try to steer clear of refined sugars. Instead, I use honey, maple syrup and the less well-known agave syrup, which has a lower glycemic index (GI) than sugar and is derived from the agave plant. It is available from most health food stores.

I also sometimes use a sugar substitute called xylitol, which is a natural sweetener, occurring in many fruits, vegetables and hardwoods, such as birch, and tastes just like sugar. Xylitol has a very low GI and helps stabilize blood sugar and insulin levels. All in all, in small amounts, xylitol is a great sugar substitute for those with a sweet tooth.

Other sugar alternatives include the extracts from the stevia leaf, which are over 100 times

sprouting chart

TYPE	DRY MEASURE	READY TO EAT	YIELDS
Almonds	1 cup	2 days	2 cups
Alfalfa Seeds	3 tablespoons	4–5 days	4 cups
Sunflower Seeds	2 cups	1–2 days	2½ cups
Sesame Seeds	1 cup	1–2 days	1½ cups
Lentils	1 cup	3 days	4 cups
Mung Beans	½ cup	2–3 days	4 cups
Chickpeas	1 cup	3 days	4 cups
Hulled Buckwheat	1 cup	1 day	2 cups
Wheat	1 cup	1 day	3 cups
Wild Rice	1 cup	1 day	3 cups

LivWise shopping list

* **lettuce** — a selection of salad leaves, bright, light and dark.
* **carrots**
* **celery**
* **tomatoes** — try to buy a variety of heirloom and cherry to use in different dishes.
* **onions** — I usually buy a variety of spring onions (scallions) and red onions.
* **beets** with the greens intact (which are great to serve, steamed, with eggs)
* **broccoli/kale/spinach/bok choy** — any or all of these can be added to a dish or steamed to make a wonderful side dish.
* **asparagus**
* **winter squash and sweet potato**
* **lemons** — buy lots of these!
* **bananas**
* **blueberries**
* **raspberries**
* **cranberries, cherries and rhubarb in season**
* **almonds**
* **oatmeal and quinoa**
* **soy milk and organic low-fat dairy milk**
* **non-fat yogurt**
* **honey** — I try to use this instead of sugar in tea. It can also help with allergies if you buy honey that is locally made from local hives.
* **maple syrup**
* **whole rye, pumpernickel or sourdough bread and crackers**
* **coconut palm sugar** (see page 16) my favorite sugar substitute!
* **olive oil and ghee**
* **sea salt and organic black pepper**
* **garlic**
* **olives**
* **Bragg Liquid Aminos** (see page 101)
* **cheese** — we love it and we eat small amounts of cheddar and love soft goat's cheese and brie.
* **butter** — love it! I have tried margarines and soy spreads over the years but I'm now back to the real thing!
* **pickled okra, dill cucumbers or peppers** — pickled or fermented foods are good for digestion.
* **coconut water** — pure and delicious!
* **English breakfast tea or green tea**
* **coffee** — organic and as locally grown as possible.
* **fish** — especially salmon and preferably locally caught from sustainable sources.
* **organic free-range chicken and eggs**
* **a bar of dark chocolate at the checkout!**

breakfast

gaia toasted muesli
serves 8

4 cups rolled oats

2 cups mixed raw, unsalted
nuts and seeds, such as
pecans, macadamia nuts or
pumpkin seeds

1 cup shredded coconut

½ cup macadamia oil

½ cup honey or raw agave syrup
(see note)

pinch sea salt

1 cup mixed currants, raisins and
dried cranberries

Preheat the oven to 375°F. Line a large baking tray with parchment paper.

Place the oats, nuts and seeds, coconut, macadamia oil, honey and salt in a large bowl and toss well to combine. Spread on the prepared baking tray and cook for about 25–30 minutes, stirring occasionally, until golden brown. Remove from the oven and allow to cool completely.

Toss the currants, cranberries and raisins through the oat mixture. Serve in bowls with milk, yogurt and fresh seasonal fruit, if desired.

Toasted muesli can be stored in an airtight container for up to 2 weeks.

Note: Raw certified organic agave syrup is a concentrated fruit juice used as a sweetener that is commercially produced from several species of the agave plant. Be careful of the brands you buy — try and get certified organic agave syrup. It is available from most health food stores.

My favorite breakfast place and indeed my favorite breakfast in the world is at Gaia. The beauty of the landscape, plus the variety of healthy and nourishing produce is awe-inspiring!

fruit salad with nut cream
serves 2

1 small banana, chopped

6 large strawberries, hulled and
chopped

¼ cup blueberries

2 kiwi fruit, chopped

1 cup chopped red papaya

1 small mango, diced

½ cup seedless red or green
grapes

2 passion fruit, pulp removed

NUT CREAM

½ cup unsalted raw cashews or
almonds

¼ cup non-dairy milk, such as oat,
almond, rice or coconut milk

To make the nut cream, put the cashews in a small bowl and pour over ¼ cup water. Cover with plastic wrap and refrigerate for at least 1 hour or overnight. Drain the nuts.

Put the nuts and milk in a food processor and process until well combined and smooth. Transfer to a bowl, cover and refrigerate until required.

To make the fruit salad, put the banana, strawberries, blueberries, kiwi fruit, papaya, mango, grapes and passion fruit pulp into a serving bowl and toss gently to combine. Serve the fruit salad with a dollop of the chilled nut cream on top.

Any leftover nut cream can be stored in an airtight container in the refrigerator for 1 day.

Note: When you are making the nut cream you can replace ¼ cup of the nuts with macadamia nuts.
You can also add a few drops of natural vanilla extract to the milk if you prefer a slightly sweeter flavor.

natural muesli
serves 8

2 cups organic rolled oats
¼ cup organic oat bran
1 cup organic wheat germ
¼ cup organic pumpkin seeds
¼ cup organic sunflower seeds
¼ cup organic golden raisins
¼ cup organic raisins
¼ cup organic dried apricots,
   finely chopped
2 organic dried figs, finely
   chopped
¼ cup organic shredded coconut

Place the oats, oat bran, wheat germ, pumpkin seeds, sunflower seeds, golden raisins, raisins, dried apricots and figs and coconut into a large bowl and toss well to combine. Add enough water just to cover the dry ingredients. Cover and refrigerate overnight.

Serve the muesli with non-dairy milk, yogurt and fresh fruit, if desired.

Natural muesli can be stored in an airtight container for up to 2 weeks.

Muesli is one of my favorite breakfast dishes. My father had it every morning of his life. It provides nourishment, energy and fiber — what could be better than that?

bircher muesli with orange and yogurt

serves 6

2 cups rolled oats

½ cup freshly squeezed orange
   juice

1 cup yogurt drink

1 cup plain yogurt

2½ tablespoons honey

1 cup golden raisins

4 oz mixed fresh fruit, such as
   banana, apple, strawberries or
   kiwi fruit

½ cup slivered almonds, toasted

Put the oats, orange juice, yogurt drink, yogurt, honey and golden raisins in a large bowl and stir well to combine. Cover with plastic wrap and refrigerate for at least 2 hours or overnight.

Just before serving, thinly slice or finely chop the fruit. Lightly fold the fruit and toasted slivered almonds through the oat mixture. Serve immediately.

Bircher muesli can be stored in an airtight container in the refrigerator for up to 1 day, but only add the fresh fruit just before serving.

poached rhubarb

serves 6–8

1 lb 10 oz rhubarb, trimmed and
    rinsed

1 vanilla bean, halved lengthwise,
    seeds scraped

1 cinnamon stick

¼ cup light palm sugar (jaggery),
    roughly chopped

4 teaspoons apple juice
    concentrate

2 teaspoons natural vanilla extract

½ cup freshly squeezed orange
    juice

Cut the rhubarb into 2½ inch lengths. Place the rhubarb into a large saucepan. Add the vanilla seeds and pod, cinnamon stick, palm sugar, apple concentrate, vanilla extract and orange juice. Add ½ cup water. Bring to a boil over high heat, then reduce the heat to low and simmer for 5–10 minutes, or until the rhubarb is soft but still holding its shape. Remove from the heat and set aside to cool.

Serve the rhubarb with plain yogurt and muesli.

Leftover rhubarb can be stored in an airtight container in the refrigerator for up to 4 days.

Ah rhubarb! This recipe is another Gaia staple that I adore. It conjures strong memories of my childhood, when my mother would cook different fruits so at any time I could open the fridge and find a tempting jar filled with delicious stewed fruit — yum!

poached eggs with cilantro pesto
serves 2

pinch sea salt

4 free-range eggs

2 slices toasted sourdough bread,
  to serve

CILANTRO PESTO
(makes 1½ cups)

2 cups firmly packed fresh cilantro
  leaves

⅔ cup extra virgin olive oil

4 garlic cloves, quartered

⅓ cup Brazil nuts

⅓ cup sunflower seeds

⅓ cup pumpkin seeds

freshly squeezed juice of 1 lemon

To make the cilantro pesto, place all the ingredients into a food processor and process to a smooth paste. Set aside. This pesto can be made ahead of time and stored in an airtight container in the refrigerator for at least 1 week. Pesto can also be frozen for up to 3 months.

Half-fill a large deep frying pan with water, add the salt and place over medium heat. Working with one egg at a time, crack the egg into a small cup. When the water is just simmering, use a large spoon to stir the water in one direction to create a whirlpool. Carefully slip the egg into the center of the whirlpool and poach for 1–2 minutes for a soft-poached egg, or until cooked to your liking. Remove with a slotted spoon to a plate, set aside and keep warm. Repeat with the remaining eggs until all are cooked.

Serve the warm poached eggs on the toast with a dollop of cilantro pesto on top.

Note: Fresh cilantro is an excellent blood purifier; 2 teaspoons of cilantro pesto every day for 3–4 weeks is known to remove heavy metals from the body. Heavy metals include mercury, lead and aluminum. This pesto also goes well with baked potatoes, pasta and rice.

Poached eggs make a great breakfast but they are so versatile that I am more than happy to eat them any time of the day — I often eat them for lunch and even a late dinner sometimes.

Livwise

bircher muesli with apple and coconut

serves 2

1 cup natural muesli (see page 26)
1 Granny Smith apple, peeled
    and coarsely grated, plus thin
    wedges of apple, extra, to
    serve (optional)
⅓ cup shredded coconut
1 cup non-dairy milk, such as oat,
    almond, rice or coconut milk
4 teaspoons xylitol (see note),
    plus extra, to serve (optional)

Put the muesli, grated apple, coconut, milk and xylitol in a bowl and stir well to combine. Cover with plastic wrap and refrigerate for at least 1 hour or overnight.

Divide the mixture between two serving bowls and serve with a little extra xylitol over the top for sweetness and the extra apple wedges if you like.

Note: Xylitol is a natural substance that is derived from fruit, vegetables and birch trees; it is also produced naturally in our bodies. Xylitol is a chemical-free, natural alternative to sugar and other artificial sweeteners. It is available from most health food stores.

Bircher muesli was a breakfast staple in our house as a child. My father made it every morning. I understand why - it is wholesome, fresh and filling - and easy to make!

protein and calcium-enriched muesli with fruit
serves 2

⅓ cup natural muesli (see page 26)

non-dairy milk, such as oat, almond, rice or coconut milk or water

2 cups chopped red papaya

2 kiwi fruit, chopped

12 strawberries, hulled and halved

¾ cup blueberries

2 passion fruit, pulp removed

2 teaspoons bee pollen (see notes)

1 teaspoon maca powder (optional) (see notes)

1 cup plain yogurt or 1 cup coconut milk

SEED AND NUT MIXTURE

4 teaspoons sunflower seeds

4 teaspoons flaxseeds

4 teaspoons pumpkin seeds

2 teaspoons sesame seeds

2 teaspoons chopped blanched almonds

2 teaspoons chopped Brazil nuts

To make the seed and nut mixture, use a spice grinder or coffee grinder to grind the seeds and nuts together until very finely chopped. Alternatively, soak all of the ingredients in just enough liquid of your choice to cover for at least 2 hours or overnight. Refrigerate until needed and drain before using.

Place the muesli and the soaking liquid in a bowl and stir well to combine. Cover with plastic wrap and refrigerate for at least 1 hour or overnight.

Put the papaya, kiwi fruit, strawberries, blueberries, passion fruit pulp, pollen, maca powder, if using, and yogurt in a bowl. Add 2 tablespoons of the seed and nut mixture and the soaked muesli and stir gently to combine. Divide between serving bowls and serve immediately.

Notes: Bee pollen contains the richest known source of vitamins (particularly B vitamins) and minerals, enzymes to aid digestion, amino acids, hormones and fats. It is available from health food stores.

Maca (*Lepidium meyenii*) is an herbaceous plant native to Peru. Maca powder is rich in essential minerals, especially selenium, calcium, magnesium and iron, and includes fatty acids including linolenic acid, palmitic acid and oleic acids, as well as polysaccharides. Maca powder is believed to improve stamina, strength and energy, and is also a hormonal tonic. It can be added to water, juice, cereals, smoothies, yogurt or herbal teas. Take ½–2 teaspoons 6 days a week (have one day off). Like superfoods, such as barley grass, wheatgrass and bee pollen, maca helps to alkalize urine, thereby helping to mobilize toxins in the body. It is available from health food stores.

strawberry and macadamia bircher muesli

serves 2

9 oz strawberries, hulled

1 cup natural muesli (see page 26)

½ cup non-dairy milk, such as oat, almond, rice or coconut milk

¼ cup macadamia nuts, chopped, plus extra, to serve

4 teaspoons xylitol (see note page 33)

Cut half of the strawberries in half. Put the cut strawberries, muesli, milk, nuts and xylitol into a bowl and stir well to combine. Cover with plastic wrap and refrigerate for at least 1 hour or overnight.

Finely chop the remaining strawberries. Divide the muesli between serving bowls and serve with the diced strawberries and extra nuts scattered on top.

The basis of muesli is oats. If you have a gluten intolerance you can replace the oats with gluten-free corn flakes, buckwheat flakes or quinoa flakes.

almond pancakes with berries and yogurt
serves 2

4½ oz strawberries, hulled and
  quartered
½ cup blueberries
⅔ cup raspberries
4 teaspoons xylitol (see note
  page 33)
mint leaves, to serve
shredded coconut, to serve
⅓ cup plain yogurt, to serve

ALMOND PANCAKES
⅔ cup ground almonds
1 teaspoon baking soda
2½ tablespoons plain yogurt
2½ tablespoons xylitol (see note
  page 33)
2 free-range eggs, lightly beaten
2 teaspoons coconut oil (see note)

Combine all of the berries in a bowl. Purée one-quarter of the mixed berries with the xylitol in a food processor or blender until smooth. Set aside.

To make the pancakes, put the ground almonds, baking soda, yogurt, xylitol, eggs and 1 tablespoon water in a mixing bowl and stir until a smooth batter forms, adding more water if needed.

Heat half of the coconut oil in a large frying pan over medium–high heat. Spoon half of the pancake mixture into the pan and cook for 2–3 minutes, or until bubbles appear on the surface. Carefully turn the pancake over and cook for a further 1–2 minutes, or until cooked through. Transfer to an ovenproof serving plate and keep warm in a low oven. Repeat with the remaining oil and pancake batter to make 2 pancakes in total.

Serve the warm almond pancakes topped with mixed berries, berry purée, mint leaves and shredded coconut. Serve with yogurt on the side.

Note: Coconut oil is available from health food stores and some grocery stores.

I love pancakes and when they are made with ground almonds, they make a healthy Sunday morning treat — the berries providing antioxidants and fiber with hardly any calories. It doesn't get much better than that!

chakchouka baked eggs
serves 4

4 teaspoons olive oil

1 small yellow onion, finely chopped

14 oz can whole tomatoes

1²/₃ cups cherry tomatoes, halved

4 teaspoons tomato paste (concentrated purée)

1 zucchini, chopped

½ red bell pepper, seeded, membrane removed and thinly sliced

½ yellow bell pepper, seeded, membrane removed and thinly sliced

½ small eggplant, chopped

1¾ cups baby spinach leaves

8 free-range eggs

Preheat the oven to 400°F.

Heat the olive oil in a large saucepan over medium–high heat. Add the onion and cook for 5 minutes, or until softened. Add the tomatoes, cherry tomatoes and tomato paste and bring to a boil. Add the zucchini, peppers and eggplant, then reduce the heat to medium–low and simmer for about 20 minutes, or until the vegetables are tender. Stir in the spinach. Transfer the vegetable mixture to a 6 cup capacity ovenproof dish. Make eight indents in the mixture to fit the eggs.

Crack the eggs into the indents in the vegetable mixture. Bake in the oven for about 10–15 minutes, or until the eggs are just set. Serve immediately.

Tip: Traditionally, Chakchouka is made with leftover vegetables from the previous night's dinner. You can also serve the Chakchouka with fresh feta cheese crumbled over the top.

steamed egg custard with shiitake mushrooms and plain yogurt

serves 4

olive oil spray, for cooking
2 fresh shiitake mushrooms, sliced
½ yellow onion, chopped
4 free-range eggs
⅔ cup plain yogurt
salt
freshly ground black pepper
2 chives, snipped, to serve
4 slices toasted soy and flaxseed
  bread, cut into fingers, to serve

Heat a frying pan over medium–high heat. Spray the pan with the oil, add the mushroom and onion, and cook for 5 minutes, or until the onion has softened. Remove from the heat and set aside.

Whisk together the eggs and yogurt, then season with salt and freshly ground black pepper. Stir through the mushroom and onion mixture.

Pour the egg mixture evenly among four ½ cup capacity ramekins or ovenproof dishes. Place the ramekins in a bamboo steamer and cover with the lid. Fill a wok one-third full with water and bring to a boil over high heat. Place the steamer in the wok (making sure it doesn't touch the water) and steam for 8 minutes, or until the custards are just set.

Sprinkle the chives over the egg custards and serve with the toast fingers on the side.

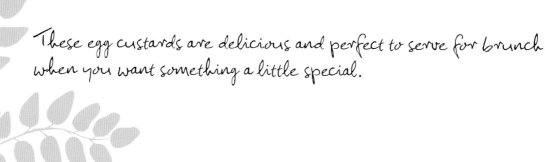

These egg custards are delicious and perfect to serve for brunch when you want something a little special.

ricotta fruit topping

makes 1 cup

¼ cup dried apricots
½ cup fresh ricotta cheese
pinch ground cinnamon

Put the dried apricots in a bowl with 1 cup water. Cover with plastic wrap and leave to soak overnight.

Drain the apricots, reserving the soaking liquid. Put the apricots and ½ cup of the soaking liquid into a blender and blend until smooth. Add the ricotta cheese and cinnamon and blend until smooth. Transfer to a bowl and serve as an accompaniment to stewed, fresh or canned fruit.

This ricotta fruit topping can be stored in an airtight container in the refrigerator for up to 2 days.

Tip: Instead of the soaked dried apricots you can try using unsweetened canned peaches and a little of their juice; or homemade stewed apple puréed with a pinch of ground cloves and 1 teaspoon honey. Alternatively you can add soaked pitted prunes and their soaking juice; or add the finely grated zest and juice of 1 orange.

baked balsamic vegetables with ricotta

serves 4

olive oil spray, for cooking

2½ tablespoons extra virgin
olive oil

2 teaspoons balsamic vinegar

2 large plum tomatoes, halved

4 large mushrooms, trimmed

1 red onion, thinly sliced

1 small fennel bulb, trimmed, cut
into ½ inch slices

2 garlic cloves, finely chopped

¼ cup crumbled fresh ricotta
cheese

4 slices toasted sourdough bread,
to serve

Preheat the oven to 350°F. Lightly grease a baking tray with the oil spray.

Whisk the olive oil and balsamic vinegar together in a small bowl until well combined.

Layer the tomato halves, mushrooms, onion, fennel, garlic and cheese on the prepared tray to create four small stacks. Drizzle with the oil mixture. Bake for 25 minutes, or until the vegetables have browned and are tender, and the cheese has melted slightly.

Serve each vegetable stack on a slice of the toasted sourdough bread.

fresh herb omelettes with balsamic mushrooms
serves 2

4 teaspoons coconut oil (see note page 36) or ghee

4½ oz button mushrooms, halved

4 teaspoons balsamic vinegar

6 free-range eggs

2½ tablespoons finely chopped flat-leaf (Italian) parsley

2½ tablespoons finely snipped chives

2½ tablespoons finely chopped basil

2½ tablespoons finely chopped thyme

mixed lettuce leaves, to serve

Heat half of the coconut oil in a frying pan over medium–high heat. Add the mushrooms and cook for about 5 minutes, stirring often, until cooked and golden brown. Remove from the heat and stir in the balsamic vinegar. Set aside and keep warm.

Put the eggs and 2 tablespoons water into a bowl and whisk until just combined. Add the herbs and mix well.

Heat 1 teaspoon of the remaining coconut oil in a frying pan over medium–high heat. Pour half of the egg mixture into the pan, swirling to coat the base. Cook for 1–2 minutes, or until almost set. Fold the omelette in half, remove to a serving plate and keep warm. Repeat with the remaining oil and egg mixture to make another omelette.

Serve the warm omelettes with the sautéed balsamic mushrooms and the lettuce leaves on the side.

John loves his eggs and this is an "easy to do" recipe.
It looks like it's difficult ... but it's not! The ingredients are something
I always have in the fridge. A great quick fix for unexpected guests
after a morning kayak!

shakes, smoothies and juices

piña colada breakfast shake
serves 1

1 cup fresh pineapple juice

1 cup coconut milk

2½ tablespoons coconut oil (see note page 36)

2½ tablespoons protein powder (see note)

¼ cup ice cubes

Put all of the ingredients into a blender and blend until the ice is crushed and the mixture is smooth. Serve immediately.

Note: When selecting a protein powder make sure it is either raw or what is called undenatured protein powder, as this type of protein powder supports the immune system. It has the ability to detoxify the cells and support cellular repair and is a very digestible source of protein. Denatured products have been heated and this process means they lose certain immunity-enhancing ingredients; many protein powders are also full of sugar. You can purchase good protein powders from most health food stores.

papaya and orange breakfast shake
serves 1

1 cup chopped red papaya

freshly squeezed juice of 1 orange

1 cup non-dairy milk, such as oat, almond, rice or coconut milk

¼ teaspoon natural vanilla extract

1 teaspoon green barley grass powder (see note)

1 teaspoon maca powder (see note page 34)

Put all of the ingredients into a blender and blend until well combined and smooth. Serve immediately.

Note: Green barley grass (*Hordeum vulgare*) powder comes from the seedling of the barley plant. It is usually harvested about 200 days after germination, when the shoots are less than 12 inches. It is a concentrated source of nearly three dozen vitamins and minerals and is particularly rich in vitamins, calcium, iron, potassium and chlorophyll. Unlike most plants, barley grass provides all nine essential amino acids (those which your body can't produce). It is available in powdered form from most health food stores.

sprouted wheat and fig smoothie
serves 1

3 dried figs, coarsely chopped
¼ cup sprouted wheat seeds
   (see page 14–15)
½ cup almond milk (see page 53)
   or other non-dairy milk, such as
   oat, rice or coconut milk

Place the figs in a small bowl. Cover with water and set aside to soak for 30 minutes, or until softened. Drain well.

Put the drained softened figs, sprouted wheat seeds and almond milk in a blender with ½ cup water and blend until well combined and smooth. Serve immediately.

apple, pear and guava juice
serves 2

2 Granny Smith apples, cored and
   quartered
2 pears, cored and quartered
2 guavas, peeled

Using an electric juice extractor, juice the apple, pear and guavas into a pitcher.

Pour into serving glasses and serve immediately.

Fresh fruit and vegetable juices are sensationally good for you, easy to make and nutritious too!

watermelon juice with maca powder
serves 4

¼ seedless watermelon, rind removed and flesh chopped
¼ teaspoon maca powder (see note page 34)

Using an electric juice extractor, juice the watermelon into a pitcher. Stir in the maca powder until well combined. Pour into serving glasses and serve immediately.

beet, celery and ginger juice
serves 1

1 large beet, including stalks and leaves, scrubbed
1 large Granny Smith apple, cored and quartered
1 celery stalk, including leaves
1 fresh ginger slice, or to taste

Using an electric juice extractor, juice the beet, apple, celery and ginger into a pitcher. Pour into a serving glass and serve immediately.

Maca powder is a whole protein from the Amazon rain forest and is a superfood providing strength, endurance and aiding in hormonal balance. It can be added to any juice combination.

spicy carrot, celery and tomato juice
serves 2

2 large carrots, halved lengthwise

3 celery stalks, including leaves, chopped

1 large tomato, quartered

pinch cayenne pepper

Using an electric juice extractor, juice the carrot, celery and tomato into a pitcher. Stir in the cayenne pepper until well combined. Pour into serving glasses and serve immediately.

spinach, broccoli and pepper juice
serves 2

4 large spinach leaves

½ cup broccoli florets

1 red pepper, seeded, membrane removed and chopped

2 Granny Smith apples, cored and quartered

1 garlic clove

Using an electric juice extractor, juice the spinach, broccoli, pepper, apple and garlic into a pitcher. Pour into serving glasses and serve immediately.

starters, snacks and breads

cornbread
makes 1 loaf

2 cups fresh corn kernels

1 teaspoon sea salt

2½ tablespoons extra virgin
   olive oil

1 cup polenta

caraway seeds (optional)

Preheat the oven to 350°F. Line the base and sides of a 4½ x 8 x 2½ inch loaf pan with parchment paper.

Put the corn in a food processor with 2 cups water and process until almost smooth. Transfer to a large bowl and add the salt, olive oil and polenta. Mix together until well combined.

Pour the mixture into the prepared pan and sprinkle the caraway seeds over the top, if using. Bake for 50 minutes, or until a knife inserted into the center of the loaf comes out clean. Allow to cool in the pan for 10 minutes, before transferring to a wire rack. Cut into slices and serve the cornbread warm or cold. Serve with your favorite spread or at breakfast with poached eggs, tomatoes, mushrooms and avocado.

This cornbread can be stored, wrapped in plastic wrap, at room temperature for up to 2 days. It can be frozen for up to 3 months. Warm the cornbread slices in a toaster or a preheated oven before serving.

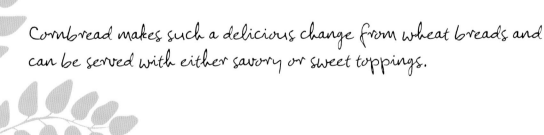

Cornbread makes such a delicious change from wheat breads and can be served with either savory or sweet toppings.

chapatti

makes 12

2 cups chickpea flour
½ teaspoon sea salt
2½ tablespoons ghee
   (clarified butter), melted

Combine the chickpea flour and salt in a large bowl and make a well in the center. Stir in ¾ cup water, or enough to mix to a soft dough. Use your hands to bring the dough together into a ball.

Turn the dough out onto a lightly floured surface and knead until the dough is smooth. Place in a lightly oiled bowl, cover with plastic wrap and set aside for 1 hour.

Divide the dough into 12 even-sized pieces. Use a rolling pin to roll each piece out on a lightly floured work surface to form circles with a 6 inch diameter, about ½ inch thick. Shake off any excess flour and set aside.

Heat a large frying pan over high heat. Brush both sides of the chapatti with the melted ghee and cook, one at a time, for about 1 minute, or until bubbles form on the surface, then turn over and cook for a further 1 minute, or until cooked through. Transfer to a serving plate and keep warm. Repeat with the remaining 11 chapatti.

Serve chapatti warm or at room temperature.

chilled watermelon gazpacho

serves 8–10

1 red pepper, seeded, membrane removed and quartered

1 yellow pepper, seeded, membrane removed and quartered

7 lb seedless watermelon

1 Lebanese (short) cucumber, cut into ¼ inch pieces

3 celery stalks, cut into ¼ inch pieces

½ small red onion, finely chopped

¼ cup mint leaves, finely chopped

5 fl oz freshly squeezed lime juice

¼ cup red wine vinegar

Preheat the broiler. Place the peppers, skin side up, on a baking sheet and cook under the broiler for about 10 minutes, or until the skin blisters and blackens. Place the pepper in a plastic bag and let stand for 10 minutes or until cooled, then peel the skin and finely chop the flesh into ¼ inch pieces.

Finely chop some of the watermelon into ¼ inch cubes and set aside — you need about 1 cup. Combine with the pepper, cucumber, celery and onion. Cover and refrigerate until required.

Chop the remaining watermelon, put into a blender and blend until smooth — you may need to do this in batches. Transfer to a large bowl and stir in the mint, lime juice and vinegar. Add half of the reserved watermelon and vegetable mixture and stir well to combine. Refrigerate the gazpacho and remaining watermelon and vegetable mixture for at least 1 hour, or until well chilled. Serve in bowls or glasses topped with the remaining watermelon and vegetable mixture.

This is so refreshing on a hot summer day and a healthy way of hydrating yourself after a long hot game of tennis under the Florida sun!

guacamole dip
makes about 2 cups

2 large avocados
½ small red onion, finely chopped
1 large plum tomato, finely
    chopped
1 garlic clove, crushed
1–2 teaspoons ground cumin,
    or to taste
1–2 teaspoons ground coriander,
    or to taste
freshly squeezed juice of 1 lemon

Halve the avocados, remove the stones and then peel. Roughly mash the flesh in a large bowl. Add the onion, tomato, garlic, cumin, coriander and lemon juice and stir well to combine.

Serve the guacamole with baked potatoes or julienne vegetables. Guacamole needs to be eaten right away and will not store for any length of time.

red kidney bean dip
makes about 3 cups

14 oz can red kidney beans
2 tomatoes, diced
worcestershire sauce, to taste
4 teaspoons tomato paste
1 red onion, finely chopped
1 garlic clove, crushed
½ teaspoon mild paprika
1 teaspoon sea salt

Put all of the ingredients into a food processor and process to make a smooth paste. Serve the red kidney bean dip with organic corn chips.

Red kidney bean dip can be stored in an airtight container in the refrigerator for 1 day.

sprouted hummus dip

makes 3 cups

1½ cups sprouted chickpeas (see
    pages 14–15)
¼ cup tahini
⅓ cup olive oil
1 cup freshly squeezed lemon
    juice
3 garlic cloves, crushed
1 teaspoon sea salt
1 teaspoon mild paprika, to serve
2½ tablespoons finely chopped
    flat-leaf (Italian) parsley,
    to serve

Put the sprouted chickpeas into an ovenproof bowl and pour over 3 cups boiling water. Set aside for at least 1 minute (this is an important step and will greatly enhance the flavor of the hummus). Drain well.

Put the sprouted chickpeas, tahini, ¼ cup of the olive oil, lemon juice, garlic and salt in a food processor and process until smooth.

Serve the sprouted hummus dip in a bowl with the remaining oil drizzled over the top. Sprinkle over the paprika and parsley, to garnish.

Note: To make a beet hummus, omit the chickpeas and add 3–4 cooked baby beets to the food processor with the remaining ingredients and process until smooth.

avocado salsa

makes 2 cups

1 large avocado
2 garlic cloves, crushed
1 small red onion, finely chopped
freshly squeezed juice of ½ lemon
1 teaspoon sea salt

Halve the avocado, remove the stone and then peel. Coarsely mash the flesh in a bowl. Add the garlic, onion, lemon juice and salt and stir well to combine.

Serve the avocado salsa with organic corn chips. The salsa is best eaten on the day it is made.

vegan cream cheese
makes 1½–2 cups

1 cup cashews
½ cup blanched almonds
¼ teaspoon sea salt
freshly squeezed juice of 1 lemon

Wash the cashews and almonds under cold running water and drain well. Place in a bowl, cover with cold water and leave to soak overnight. Drain well.

Put all of the ingredients into a food processor with ¾ cup water and process until the mixture is well combined and smooth.

Transfer the mixture to a squeeze bottle as this will help when serving. Drizzle it over pizza Italiano (see page 123) or use it to dress a salad.

Vegan cream cheese can be stored in an airtight container in the refrigerator for up to 10 days.

vegan parmesan cheese
makes about 1 cup

5½ oz Brazil nuts or hazelnuts
1 garlic clove, chopped
1 pinch sea salt

Put all of the ingredients into a food processor and process until finely chopped.

Vegan parmesan cheese is used in the salad topping on the pizza Italiano (see page 123), or can be added to any basic salad. It can be stored in an airtight container in the freezer for up to 3 months.

cracker bread
makes about 20 pieces

1½ cups sprouted wheat (see pages 14–15)
1 teaspoon sea salt

Put the sprouted wheat, sea salt and ¼ cup water in a food processor and process to make a smooth paste, adding more water if necessary.

Pour the mixture evenly over plastic dehydrator sheets. Set the dehydrator temperature to low. Place in the dehydrator and dehydrate for about 24 hours, or until the bread lifts away from the dehydrator sheets.

Note: You can sprinkle your favorite herbs, seeds or spices over the top of cracker breads before dehydrating. Cracker bread can be stored in an airtight container for up to 1 week.

salads and dressings

quinoa salad
serves 4

1 cup quinoa
½ cup sunflower seeds
4 teaspoons tamari or soy sauce
2 Lebanese (short) cucumbers, diced
1 cup shredded red cabbage
4 scallions, thinly sliced
1¾ cups baby spinach leaves

SPICY TAHINI DRESSING
¼ cup tahini
freshly squeezed juice of 1 lemon
4 teaspoons white miso paste
2 garlic cloves, crushed
pinch cayenne pepper

To make the spicy tahini dressing, put all of the ingredients into a small bowl with ¼ cup water. Whisk well until smooth and combined. Set aside until needed.

Put the quinoa and 2 cups water in a small saucepan over high heat. Bring to a boil, then reduce the heat to low, cover, and simmer for 10–15 minutes, or until the quinoa is tender and all of the water has been absorbed. Remove from the heat, transfer to a large bowl and cool.

Meanwhile, dry-fry the sunflower seeds in a frying pan over medium heat for 1 minute, or until aromatic. Add the tamari to the pan, then remove from the heat and stir well to coat the seeds. Add to the quinoa with the cucumber, cabbage, scallion and spinach and toss gently to combine. Drizzle over the spicy tahini dressing and toss well before serving.

Salads are a staple at my house — I always keep salad supplies in the fridge so I can whip up an easy lunch at short notice.

coleslaw with cashew nut dressing
serves 4

¼ red cabbage, shredded

¼ green cabbage, shredded

2 large carrots, grated

2 celery stalks, thinly sliced

1 red pepper, seeded, membrane
    removed and sliced

1 large red onion, thinly sliced

3½ oz chopped pineapple

CASHEW NUT DRESSING

½ cup cashew nuts

freshly squeezed juice of ½ lemon

½ teaspoon garlic powder (see note)

pinch sea salt

To make the cashew nut dressing, soak the cashews in ½ cup water for at least 1 hour. Drain well.

Put the cashews into a food processor with the remaining ingredients and process until well combined and almost smooth. Set aside until needed.

Just before you are ready to serve, put all of the salad ingredients and the dressing into a large serving bowl and toss gently to combine.

Note: Garlic powder is made from ground dehydrated garlic. It is available from most health food stores and any supermarket.

Traditional coleslaw is made with green cabbage. I like combining the red and green and adding the onion and red pepper for added flavor and color - the pineapple is a fun touch! Very Aussie!

gaia gado gado salad
serves 6

1 lb 5 oz firm tofu, cut into ½ inch cubes

2 lemongrass stems, white part only, thinly sliced

2 garlic cloves, lightly crushed

¼ cup macadamia oil

1 large carrot, thinly sliced

¼ Chinese cabbage, shredded

1 lb 2 oz baby bok choy, shredded

1 Lebanese (short) cucumber, sliced

½ pineapple, peeled, cored and chopped

3 scallions, sliced

1 cup cilantro leaves

4 long red chiles, seeded and thinly sliced

GADO GADO DRESSING

¾ cup macadamia nuts or peanuts, lightly toasted

freshly squeezed juice of 3 limes

⅓ cup kecap manis (see note)

⅓ cup coconut milk

4 teaspoons fish sauce

1 garlic clove, crushed

Put the tofu, lemongrass, garlic and macadamia oil into a bowl. Cover with plastic wrap and refrigerate overnight.

To make the gado gado dressing, put the macadamia nuts into a food processor and process until they resemble fine breadcrumbs. Transfer to a bowl and stir in the lime juice, kecap manis, coconut milk, fish sauce and garlic. Set aside until needed.

Cook the carrot in a small saucepan of boiling water for 2 minutes, or until tender. Refresh in cold water, drain well and set aside.

Cook the tofu on a barbecue hot plate or in a frying pan over medium heat for 2–3 minutes, turning often, until golden brown — the lemongrass should be a little crunchy.

Put the carrot and remaining salad ingredients into a large bowl and toss well to combine. Add the gado gado dressing and gently toss again before serving. Place the tofu on top.

Note: Kecap manis may be found in specialty Asian groceries. As a substitute, combine cup cup soy sauce with 3 teaspoons brown sugar, grated palm sugar, or honey.

garden salad
serves 2

½ red pepper, halved, seeded
   and membrane removed
2 teaspoons olive oil
2 garlic cloves, crushed
2 cups mixed salad leaves
1 carrot, coarsely grated
1 beetroot, trimmed, peeled and
   coarsely grated
6 cherry tomatoes, halved
¼ red onion, thinly sliced
4 sun-dried tomatoes, chopped
1 avocado, peeled, stone
   removed and flesh diced
½ cup mung bean sprouts
¼ cup basil, mint or Italian (flat-
   leaf) parsley, finely chopped
salad dressing of your choice,
   to serve (see pages 102–107)

Preheat the oven to 400°F. Line a baking sheet with parchment paper.

Place the pepper halves on the prepared sheet. Drizzle with the oil and sprinkle with garlic. Bake for 20 minutes, or until tender. When cool enough to handle, cut the pepper into thick strips.

Divide the pepper and remaining ingredients between two serving bowls and toss gently to combine. Drizzle the dressing over the salad and serve immediately.

Note: Try adding some crumbled goat's cheese or fresh mozzarella cheese for extra flavor — delicious!

My husband, John, calls my salads "kitchen roulette" because I never make them the same way twice! I tend to use whatever is in the fridge and just add one of my favorite dressings.

mung bean salad
serves 2

2 cups mung bean sprouts
2 teaspoons coconut oil (see note
    page 36)
1 large yellow onion, thinly sliced
2 garlic cloves, crushed
1 teaspoon grated fresh ginger
¼ cup shoyu (Japanese soy sauce)
2 tablespoons brown rice vinegar
    (see note)
1 teaspoon sesame oil

Put the mung bean sprouts in a colander and pour boiling water over them. Drain well.

Heat the coconut oil in a large frying pan over medium–high heat. Cook the onion, garlic and ginger for about 5 minutes, or until softened. Add the soy sauce, rice vinegar and sesame oil and cook for a further 2 minutes, stirring well to combine. Remove from the heat and stir in the sprouts. Transfer to a serving bowl and serve immediately.

Note: You can also serve this salad on a bed of steamed rice or with lightly pan-fried tofu.

Brown rice vinegar is available from health food stores.

carrot salad with papaya and orange dressing
serves 2

2 large carrots, coarsely grated
⅓ cup pine nuts, toasted
⅓ cup golden raisins

PAPAYA AND ORANGE DRESSING
1 cup chopped red papaya
½ cup freshly squeezed
    orange juice
½ cup olive oil
pinch sea salt

To make the papaya and orange dressing place all of the ingredients into a blender and blend until smooth. Set aside until needed.

Put all of the salad ingredients and the dressing into a large serving bowl and toss gently to combine. Serve immediately.

tabouleh and avocado salad
serves 4

½ cup bulgur

1 celery stalk, thinly sliced

1 Lebanese (short) cucumber, cut into ½ inch cubes

2 large plum tomatoes, seeded and cut into ½ inch cubes

2 large avocados, peeled, stones removed and flesh thinly sliced

8 scallions, thinly sliced

1 bunch flat-leaf (Italian) parsley, leaves finely chopped

1 bunch mint, leaves finely chopped

LEMON VINEGAR DRESSING

½ cup olive oil

freshly squeezed juice of 2 lemons

finely grated zest of 2 lemons

2½ tablespoons white wine vinegar

1 garlic clove, crushed

pinch sea salt

pinch xylitol (see note page 33)

2 teaspoons Dijon mustard (optional)

Put the bulgur in a bowl and pour over enough boiling water to cover by 2 inches. Set aside to soak for 10–15 minutes, or until tender. Drain well.

Meanwhile, to make the lemon vinegar dressing put all of the ingredients into a jar and shake well to combine. Set aside until needed.

Put the drained bulgur in a large bowl with the celery, cucumber, tomatoes, avocados, scallions, parsley and mint. Add ⅓ cup of the lemon vinegar dressing and toss gently to combine.

Divide the salad between serving bowls and drizzle with the remaining dressing, to serve.

salads and dressings

squash and beet salad with mustard dressing

serves 4

3 lbs baby beets

4 teaspoons olive oil

1 lb butternut squash

½ cup walnuts, toasted

4 cups mixed salad leaves

1¾ cups baby spinach leaves

1 Lebanese cucumber, halved
   lengthwise and sliced

8 cherry tomatoes, halved

1 cup basil

4 scallions, thinly sliced

½ cup sunflower sprouts

MUSTARD DRESSING

⅓ cup olive oil

2½ tablespoons white vinegar

1 tablespoon honey

1 teaspoon whole grain mustard

1 teaspoon Di jon mustard

Preheat the oven to 325°F.

Trim the beet leaves, leaving ¾ inch of the stems attached. Gently scrub the beet bulbs and pat dry with paper towels. Put into a large bowl, drizzle with half of the olive oil and toss to coat. Wrap each beet in foil, place in a large roasting pan and bake for 1 hour, or until tender when tested with a knife.

Meanwhile, peel the squash, discarding the seeds and cut into small wedges. Place in a roasting pan and lightly coat in the remaining oil. Bake for 25–30 minutes, or until tender and lightly golden.

To make the mustard dressing, combine all of the ingredients in a jar and shake well to combine.

Put the walnuts, salad leaves, spinach, cucumber, tomatoes, basil, scallions and sunflower sprouts into a large bowl. Add the mustard dressing and toss well to coat. Serve the salad with the roasted beets and squash.

There is something very homey and earthy about root vegetables — this recipe is easy and brings out the best of these vegetable flavors — scrumptious!

asparagus, chickpea and potato salad with yogurt and mint dressing

serves 2

6 oz small new potatoes
6 oz asparagus spears, trimmed
  and cut into 1¼ inch lengths
3 cups baby spinach leaves
14 oz can chickpeas, rinsed
  and drained
¼ cup pumpkin seeds, toasted

YOGURT AND MINT DRESSING
¼ cup sheep's milk yogurt
finely grated zest of ½ lime
freshly squeezed juice of ½ lime
freshly squeezed juice of ½ lemon
¼ cup mint leaves, finely chopped
pinch sea salt

To make the yogurt and mint dressing, put all of the ingredients into a blender and blend until smooth. Cover with plastic wrap and place in the refrigerator until needed.

Cook the potatoes in a large saucepan of boiling water for 10 minutes, or until tender. Add the asparagus to the pan for the last 2 minutes and cook until bright green and tender. Rinse the asparagus immediately under cold water and drain well. Cut the potatoes in half and cool.

Put the spinach, chickpeas, pumpkin seeds, asparagus, potato halves and dressing in a large serving bowl and toss gently to combine. Serve immediately with the yogurt and mint dressing drizzled over the top.

This yogurt and mint dressing also tastes great spooned over baked potatoes — a whole meal in itself!

green papaya salad
serves 4

1 green papaya, flesh chopped

2 small plum tomatoes, diced

½ cup macadamia nuts, chopped

¼ teaspoon cayenne pepper

2½ tablespoons finely chopped
   cilantro leaves

DRESSING

freshly squeezed juice of ½ lemon

3 garlic cloves, crushed

4 teaspoons soy sauce

4 teaspoons agave syrup (see
   note page 22)

To make the dressing, put all of the ingredients into a jar and shake until well combined. Set aside until needed.

Just before you are ready to serve, put all of the salad ingredients into a large serving bowl with the dressing and toss gently to combine. Serve immediately.

tuna niçoise salad with Olivia's favorite dressing

serves 2

6 oz small new potatoes

¼ lb green beans

2 x ¼ lb tuna steaks

olive oil spray, for cooking

1 small red onion, thinly sliced

2 hard-boiled free-range eggs,
    quartered

2 cups mixed salad leaves

8 cherry tomatoes, halved

flat-leaf (Italian) parsley,
    to garnish

OLIVIA'S FAVORITE DRESSING

freshly squeezed juice of ½ lemon

2½ tablespoons olive oil

½ teaspoon Bragg Liquid Aminos,
    or to taste (see note)

To make Olivia's favorite dressing, put the lemon juice, olive oil and the Bragg Liquid Aminos in a jar and shake well to combine. Taste and add more liquid aminos if preferred. Set aside until needed.

Cook the potatoes in a large saucepan of boiling water for 10 minutes, or until tender. Add the beans to the pan for the last 2 minutes of cooking, or until bright green and tender. Rinse the beans immediately under cold water and drain well. Halve the potatoes and set aside to cool.

Spray both sides of the tuna with the oil spray. Sear the tuna on a barbecue hot plate for 2 minutes on each side for medium, or until cooked to your liking. Transfer to a plate and set aside to rest for 2–3 minutes.

Arrange the potato halves on serving plates with the beans, onion, egg, salad leaves and tomato. Top with the tuna and drizzle the dressing over the top. Garnish with the parsley, to serve.

Note: Bragg Liquid Aminos is a certified non-GMO liquid protein concentrate. It is made from soybeans and contains essential and non-essential amino acids. It is available from most health food stores.

You can replace the tuna steaks in this recipe with a 15 oz can of tuna in springwater or olive oil. Drain well and flake into large chunks before adding to the salad.

basic vinaigrette

makes ⅔ cup

¼ cup olive oil

¼ cup white wine vinegar

4 teaspoons Dijon or
whole grain mustard

1 garlic clove, crushed

4 teaspoons finely chopped
flat-leaf (Italian) parsley,
oregano or rosemary

Put all of the ingredients into a jar and shake well to combine.

Any leftover dressing can be stored in an airtight container in
the refrigerator for up to 1 week.

gaia classic vinaigrette dressing

makes ⅔ cup

¼ cup apple cider vinegar

¼ cup olive, macadamia,
grapeseed or sunflower oil

4 teaspoons Dijon or whole
grain mustard

4 teaspoons honey or agave syrup
(see note page 22)

Put all of the ingredients into a jar and shake well to combine.

Any leftover dressing can be stored in an airtight container in
the refrigerator for up to 10 days.

gaia raspberry vinaigrette
makes ½ cup

2 tablespoons raspberry vinegar
2 tablespoons verjuice (see note)
⅓ cup macadamia or grapeseed
    oil

Put all of the ingredients into a jar and shake well to combine.

Any leftover dressing can be stored in an airtight container in the refrigerator for up to 2 weeks.

Note: Verjuice is a milder form of vinegar. It is made from unripened grapes and adds fruity undertones. It is available from most specialty grocery stores and delicatessens.

white wine vinegar and olive oil dressing
makes 1 cup

⅓ cup white wine vinegar
⅔ cup olive oil
½ teaspoon dried oregano

Put all of the ingredients into a jar and shake well to combine.

Any leftover dressing can be stored in an airtight container in the refrigerator for up to 1 week.

My husband, John, is a 'sauceaholic' — he gets very excited about the tasty addition that salad dressings and vinaigrettes add to our mealtimes.

entrées

bush-spiced fish with sweet potato mash and fruit salsa

serves 4

1 lb orange sweet potato, chopped

2 inch piece fresh ginger, finely grated

2 oz dukkah (see note)

6 oz skinless firm white fish fillets

4 teaspoons olive oil

lime wedges, to serve

FRUIT SALSA

½ small red onion, finely chopped

1 kiwi fruit, finely chopped

1 small mango, finely chopped

¼ small pineapple, cored and finely chopped

2½ tablespoons finely chopped cilantro leaves

freshly squeezed juice of 1 lime

2½ tablespoons olive oil

1 teaspoon Tabasco sauce, or to taste

To make the fruit salsa, put all of the ingredients into a bowl and stir to combine. Cover with plastic wrap and refrigerate until needed.

Preheat the oven to 400°F. Line a baking sheet with parchment paper.

Cook the sweet potato in a large saucepan of boiling water for 15 minutes, or until tender. Drain well and mash together with the ginger; season with sea salt and freshly ground black pepper. Set aside and keep warm.

Sprinkle the dukkah over the fish fillets. Heat the oil in a large frying pan over medium heat and cook the fish for about 5 minutes on each side, or until lightly golden on both sides. Transfer the fish to the prepared sheet and bake for 8–10 minutes, or until just cooked through.

Divide the sweet potato mash between serving plates, top with the fish fillets and spoon some of the fruit salsa over the top. Serve with lime wedges.

Note: Dukkah is a ground nut, seed and spice mixture that is often used as a condiment and flavoring. The version we use at Gaia includes pecans, wattleseeds, hazelnuts, macadamia nuts, sesame seeds, salt, lemon myrtle and coriander. Dukkah is available from some health food stores and specialty grocery stores.

spicy dhal
serves 6–8

2 cups red lentils, rinsed

½ cup jasmine rice, rinsed

7 oz coconut milk

1 carrot, finely diced

¼ small cauliflower, cut into
small florets

1 cinnamon stick

1 bay leaf

1 tablespoon yellow curry paste

¼ teaspoon green curry paste

1 teaspoon sea salt

1 tablespoon boiling water

2 oz baby spinach leaves

½ cup frozen peas

1 teaspoon olive oil

½ teaspoon fennel seeds

½ teaspoon cumin seeds

½ teaspoon ground turmeric

½ teaspoon ground coriander

½ teaspoon vegetable stock
bouillon (powder)

½ teaspoon xylitol (see note
page 33)

½ teaspoon freshly ground
black pepper

Greek-style yogurt, to serve

Put the lentils, rice and 4 cups water in a large saucepan over high heat. Bring to a boil, then reduce the heat to medium–low, add the coconut milk, carrot, cauliflower, cinnamon stick and bay leaf and simmer, uncovered, for 15 minutes.

Put the yellow and green curry pastes in a small bowl with ½ teaspoon of the sea salt and the boiling water and stir well to combine. Add to the lentil mixture and cook, stirring occasionally, for a further 15 minutes, or until the lentils are tender. Stir in the spinach and peas and cook for 3 minutes, or until the spinach has wilted and is bright green. Discard the cinnamon stick and bay leaf.

Meanwhile, heat the olive oil in a small frying pan over high heat. Add the fennel seeds, cumin seeds, turmeric and coriander and cook for 30 seconds, or until aromatic. Transfer to a bowl and add the bouillon, xylitol, remaining salt and the pepper and stir to combine.

Serve the warm dhal with the seeds and spices sprinkled over the top and the yogurt on the side.

carrot cashew soup
serves 4–6

1 cup cashew nuts
2½ tablespoons macadamia oil
2 yellow onions, coarsely chopped
3 inch piece fresh ginger, finely
  chopped
2½ lbs carrots, coarsely chopped
pinch cayenne pepper, or to taste
fresh cilantro leaves, to serve

Rinse the cashews under cold running water and drain. Place in a bowl and pour over enough water to cover, then set aside and soak overnight. Drain well.

Heat the macadamia oil in a large saucepan over medium–high heat. Add the onion and ginger and cook for about 5 minutes, or until the onion softens. Add the cashews, carrots and 6 cups water. Bring to a boil, then reduce the heat to medium–low and simmer, uncovered, for about 15 minutes, or until the carrots are tender. Stir in the cayenne pepper, then remove from the heat and allow to cool slightly.

Transfer the soup to a food processor or blender and process, in batches, until smooth. Return the soup to the pan over medium heat until heated through. Serve topped with the cilantro leaves.

John and I love all orange vegetables and this soup satisfies that and our love of hot and spicy! And it's nutritious too!

Olivia's lemon chicken

serves 4–6

3 lbs organic chicken
1 large lemon
2½ tablespoons olive oil or
   melted butter
roasted orange sweet potato,
   to serve
steamed broccoli or green salad,
   to serve

Preheat the oven to 400°F. Lightly grease a roasting pan and place a wire rack in the base of the pan.

Trim any excess fat from the chicken and discard the neck. Rinse the chicken (including the cavity) under cold running water and pat dry with paper towel. Season the cavity with sea salt and freshly ground black pepper.

Using a fork or metal skewer, prick the lemon all over and place inside the chicken cavity. Rub the oil all over the outside of the chicken and season well. Roast the chicken for 45 minutes–1 hour, or until the juices run clear when the thigh is pierced with a knife. Remove from the oven and allow to rest, covered, for 10 minutes before serving.

Serve the roast chicken with orange sweet potato, the steamed broccoli or a green salad.

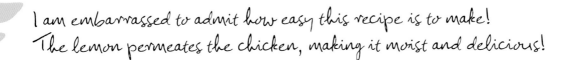

I am embarrassed to admit how easy this recipe is to make! The lemon permeates the chicken, making it moist and delicious!

mexican chili beef tacos

serves 6

2 yellow onions, finely chopped

1 garlic clove, crushed

1¼ lbs lean ground beef

2 beef bouillon cubes

2½ tablespoons tomato paste

2 teaspoons chili powder

½ teaspoon ground cumin

½ teaspoon ground coriander

½ teaspoon dried oregano

14 oz can red kidney beans,
   drained

12 taco shells

shredded lettuce, to serve

grated low-fat cheddar cheese,
   to serve

finely chopped tomatoes, to serve

diced avocado, to serve

Heat 2 tablespoons water in a large frying pan over medium heat. Add the onion and garlic and cook for 4 minutes, or until the onion softens. Add the beef, increase the heat to medium–high and cook for 5 minutes, breaking up any large lumps of meat with a spoon, until the meat has browned. Add the bouillon cubes, tomato paste, chile powder, cumin, coriander, oregano and 2 cups water and stir until well combined. Bring to a boil over high heat, then reduce the heat to low and simmer for 30 minutes, or until thickened.

Add the kidney beans and stir to combine. Bring the mixture to a boil, then remove from the heat and keep warm.

Heat the taco shells following the packet directions. Place on a platter with the lettuce, cheese, tomato and avocado. Serve the chili beef in a bowl and allow guests to assemble their own tacos.

Always a favorite. Try flour tortillas or lavash instead of tacos to reduce the fat and calorie count.

ocean trout on pea and yogurt mash
serves 4

3 cups fresh or frozen green peas

1 large yellow onion, chopped

1¾ cups Greek-style yogurt

4 x 6 oz skinless, boneless ocean
trout or salmon fillets

4 teaspoons olive oil

4 teaspoons chopped flat-leaf
(Italian) parsley

4 teaspoons snipped chives

4 teaspoons chopped mint

Cook the peas and onion in a saucepan of boiling water for 2–4 minutes, or until tender. Use a fork to mash together the peas and onion, then stir through ¾ cup of the yogurt. Set aside and keep warm until ready to serve.

Brush the fish lightly on both sides with the oil and cook on a preheated stovetop grill or frying pan over medium–high heat for 3 minutes on each side, or until almost cooked through.

Serve the fish with the pea and yogurt mash on the side and a dollop of the remaining yogurt on top. Sprinkle with the combined herbs and season with freshly ground black pepper.

This is a healthy meal option that's quick to make but makes an impact at a dinner party as well.

chickpea patties
makes 8 (serves 4)

1 lb 5 oz all-purpose potatoes

2 x 14 oz cans chickpeas, rinsed
 and drained

1 carrot, grated

1 yellow onion, finely chopped

1 garlic clove, crushed

¼ cup cilantro leaves, finely
 chopped

2 teaspoons vegetable bouillon

½ teaspoon sea salt

4 teaspoons sunflower seeds,
 ground

2½ tablespoons tahini

1 free-range egg

¼ cup fine polenta

olive oil, for frying

Preheat the oven to 400°F. Line a baking sheet with parchment paper.

Peel and slice the potatoes. Cook them in a saucepan of boiling water for 15 minutes, or until very tender. Drain well. Mash in a large bowl until smooth and then allow to cool.

Add the chickpeas, carrot, onion, garlic, cilantro, bouillon, salt, ground sunflower seeds and tahini to the mashed potato. Mash the ingredients together until well combined. Add the egg and stir well to combine.

Take half a cup of mixture at a time and shape into patties. Roll the patties in the polenta to coat lightly and set aside on the prepared sheet.

Heat a little olive oil in a large frying pan over medium–high heat. Cook the patties, in batches, for about 2 minutes on each side, or until golden brown. Return the patties to the prepared sheet and bake in the oven for about 20 minutes, or until heated through. Serve with your favorite salad and dressing (see pages 80–107).

pizza italiano
serves 2

1 oz arugula leaves

1 small carrot, coarsely grated

2½ tablespoons sun-dried
   tomatoes

¼ red onion, thinly sliced

¼ red pepper, seeded, membrane
   removed and cut into thin strips

⅓ cup sprouted sunflower seeds
   (see pages 14–15)

4 teaspoons basil leaves, torn

2 teaspoons pine nuts

3 cherry tomatoes, quartered

1½–2½ tablespoons vegan
   parmesan cheese (see page 76)

1 pizza crust (see page 70)

2½ tablespoons tahini

½ quantity avocado salsa (see
   page 75)

2½ tablespoons pesto (see
   page 71)

1 plum tomato, thinly sliced

vegan cream cheese (see
   page 76), to serve

Put the arugula, carrot, sun-dried tomatoes, onion, pepper, sunflower sprouts, basil, pine nuts, cherry tomatoes and vegan parmesan cheese into a large bowl and toss to combine.

Spread the pizza crust with tahini, avocado salsa and pesto. Top with tomato slices and the combined vegetables. Serve with the vegan cream cheese spooned over the top.

124

mushroom soup with lemon and thyme

serves 4

4 teaspoons extra virgin olive oil

1 large yellow onion, coarsely
  chopped

2 garlic cloves, crushed

10½ oz mixed mushrooms,
  coarsely chopped

3¼ oz dry white wine

2 all-purpose potatoes, chopped

4 cups vegetable stock

2 teaspoons thyme leaves,
  plus extra sprigs (optional),
  to garnish

1–2 teaspoons finely grated
  lemon zest

1 bay leaf

Heat the olive oil in a large saucepan over high heat. Add the onion, garlic and mushrooms and cook for about 5 minutes, or until the onion softens. Add the wine and simmer until it has almost evaporated.

Add the potato, stock, thyme, lemon zest and bay leaf and bring to a boil. Reduce the heat to medium–low and simmer, uncovered, for 15 minutes, or until the potato is tender. Remove from the heat and allow to cool slightly. Discard the bay leaf.

Transfer the soup to a food processor or blender, in batches, and process until smooth. Return the soup to the pan over medium heat until warm. Serve immediately, garnished with thyme sprigs, if desired.

This soup is a beautiful combination of mushrooms, lemon and thyme. The soup has an amazing array of earthy flavors and is a favorite at Gaia. We use only organic ingredients when making this delicious soup.

walnut patties
serves 4

1 cup ground walnuts

1 cup cooked brown rice

¼ cup spelt flour

1 cup fresh breadcrumbs

½ teaspoon sea salt

½ teaspoon dried sage

1 garlic clove, crushed

2 teaspoons vegetable bouillon

¼ cup almond butter
  (see note)

2½ tablespoons soy sauce

olive oil, for frying

Preheat the oven to 400°F. Line a baking sheet with parchment paper.

Put the ground walnuts, cooked rice, flour, breadcrumbs, salt, sage, garlic, bouillon, almond butter and soy sauce into a large bowl and stir well to combine. Set aside for about 15 minutes.

Take one-quarter of a cup of mixture at a time and shape it into patties. Repeat to make 10 patties in total.

Heat a little olive oil in a large frying pan over medium–high heat. Cook the patties, in batches, for 2 minutes on each side, or until golden brown. Transfer to the prepared sheet and bake for about 10 minutes, or until heated through.

Serve the walnut patties with your favorite salad and dressing (see pages 80–107).

Note: Almond butter is made from almonds that are blended to make a paste. It is available from selected supermarkets and health food stores.

chickpea casserole
serves 6–8

4 teaspoons olive oil

1 large yellow onion, diced

1 red pepper, seeded, membrane
removed and diced

2 garlic cloves, crushed

1 teaspoon dried oregano

2 cups chopped tomatoes

4 teaspoons tomato paste

2 x 14 oz cans chickpeas, rinsed
and drained

1 carrot, diced

2 large potatoes, diced

1 teaspoon sea salt

4 teaspoons vegetable bouillon

2½ tablespoons chopped flat-leaf
(Italian) parsley

Heat the oil in a large saucepan over medium–high heat. Add the onion, pepper, garlic and oregano and cook for about 5 minutes, stirring often, until the onion softens.

Add the tomatoes, tomato paste, chickpeas, carrot, potatoes, salt, bouillon and enough water to just cover the vegetables. Bring to a boil, then reduce the heat to medium–low and simmer, partially covered, for 25–30 minutes. Remove from the heat, stir in the parsley and serve immediately.

veggie patties
serves 6 (makes about 12)

14 oz all-purpose potatoes,
   coarsely grated

1 large zucchini, coarsely grated

1 large onion, coarsely grated

14 oz orange sweet potatoes,
   peeled and coarsely grated

1 carrot, coarsely grated

1 garlic clove, crushed

2 teaspoons finely grated fresh
   ginger

1 cup flat-leaf (Italian) parsley,
   finely chopped

½ teaspoon ground coriander

½ teaspoon dried rosemary

½ teaspoon dried oregano

½ teaspoon sea salt

3 free-range eggs, lightly beaten

¾ cup spelt flour

olive oil, for cooking

Preheat the oven to 400°F. Line a baking sheet with parchment paper.

Put the potatoes, zucchini and onion in a colander and use your hands to squeeze out as much moisture as possible. Put these into a large bowl and add the sweet potato, carrot, garlic, ginger, parsley, coriander, rosemary, oregano, salt, eggs and ½ cup of the flour and stir until well combined. Cover and set aside for 15 minutes.

Take one-quarter of a cup of the mixture at a time and push the mixture into a patty shape. Roll in the remaining flour to coat both sides. Repeat with the remaining mixture to make about 12 in total.

Heat a little olive oil in a large frying pan over medium–high heat. Cook the patties, in batches, for 3–4 minutes on each side, or until golden brown. Transfer to the prepared sheet and bake for about 20 minutes, or until cooked through. Serve the patties with your favorite salad and dressing (see pages 80–107).

Note: This mixture may be a little wet and therefore a little difficult to shape, however the moisture will add to the lightness of these patties.

These are great cold the next day – we love to take them with some crunchy bread, mustard and John's favorite sauces for a picnic at the beach!

lentil and spinach casserole
serves 6–8

4 teaspoons olive oil

1 yellow onion, finely chopped

2 garlic cloves, crushed

1 red pepper, seeded, membrane
   removed and diced

1 teaspoon sea salt

2 teaspoons ground coriander

¼ teaspoon asafetida powder
   (see note)

¼ teaspoon cayenne pepper

4 teaspoons vegetable bouillon

4 ripe tomatoes, chopped

4 teaspoons tomato paste

14 oz can brown lentils, rinsed
   and drained

1 carrot, diced

2 large all-purpose potatoes,
   diced

juice of ½ lemon

1 teaspoon xylitol (see note
   page 33)

2½ tablespoons chopped flat-leaf
   (Italian) parsley

5 spinach leaves, shredded

steamed rice or chapatti (see
   page 67), to serve

Heat the oil in a large, heavy-based saucepan over medium–high heat. Add the onion, garlic and pepper and cook for about 5 minutes, stirring often, until the onion softens. Add the salt, coriander, asafetida powder, cayenne pepper and bouillon and cook, stirring, for 1 minute, or until aromatic.

Add the tomatoes, tomato paste, lentils, carrot, potatoes, lemon juice, xylitol and enough water to just cover the vegetables. Bring to a boil, then reduce the heat to medium–low and simmer, covered, for 25–30 minutes. Remove from the heat and stir in the parsley and spinach leaves. Serve with steamed rice or chapatti.

Note: Asafetida powder is used widely in Indian cooking and is a powdered flavoring obtained from a large, fennel-like plant. Because of its pungency, it is always used in small quantities. It is available from Indian grocery stores and some health food stores.

zucchini and carrot patties
serves 4

1 large zucchini, grated

3 cups grated carrot

¾ cup spelt flour

1 yellow onion, finely chopped

1 garlic clove, crushed

¼ cup flat-leaf (Italian) parsley,
   finely chopped

¼ teaspoon dried rosemary

¼ teaspoon kelp powder
   (see note)

½ teaspoon sea salt

3 free-range eggs, lightly beaten

½ cup wheat germ

coconut oil (see note page 36),
   for frying

Preheat the oven to 400°F. Line a baking sheet with parchment paper.

Put the zucchini, carrot, flour, onion, garlic, parsley, rosemary, kelp powder, salt and eggs into a large bowl and stir well until completely combined.

Take half a cup of mixture at a time and shape into a large patty. Roll in the wheat germ to coat on both sides. Repeat with the remaining mixture to make 10 patties in total.

Heat a little coconut oil in a large frying pan over medium–low heat. Cook the patties, in batches, for 2 minutes on each side, or until browned all over. Transfer to the prepared sheet and bake for about 10 minutes, or until cooked through. Serve the zucchini and carrot patties with your favorite salad and dressing (see pages 80–107).

Note: Kelp is a sea vegetable packed with nutrients, particularly iodine. Iodine helps the thyroid to function correctly and is also known to support the immune system. Kelp powder is available from health food stores.

navy bean and rice bake
serves 6

4 teaspoons coconut oil
  (see note page 36)
1 large yellow onion, finely
  chopped
1 garlic clove, crushed
4 large ripe tomatoes, chopped
2 x 14 oz cans navy beans, rinsed
  and drained
1 cup cooked brown rice
1 cup flat-leaf (Italian) parsley,
  finely chopped
1 vegetarian bouillon cube
1 teaspoon sea salt
1 teaspoon thyme leaves
cayenne pepper, to taste
1 cup fresh breadcrumbs
2½ tablespoons ground almonds

Preheat the oven to 350°F. Lightly grease a 6 cup capacity baking dish.

Heat the coconut oil in a large saucepan over high heat. Add the onion and garlic and cook for about 5 minutes, or until the onion softens. Add the tomatoes, beans, rice, parsley, bouillon cube, salt, thyme and ½ cup water. Cook for 15–20 minutes, stirring occasionally, or until thickened slightly. Season to taste with the cayenne pepper.

Transfer the bean mixture to the prepared dish and sprinkle with the combined breadcrumbs and ground almonds. Bake for about 30 minutes, or until golden. Remove from the oven and allow to stand for 10 minutes before serving.

potato and lentil pie
serves 8

SPELT PASTRY

¾ cup spelt flour
¾ cup self-rising spelt flour
½ teaspoon salt
2½ tablespoons olive oil

LENTIL FILLING

4 teaspoons olive oil
1 small yellow onion, finely chopped
2 garlic cloves, crushed
½ red pepper, seeded, membrane
    removed and finely chopped
4 button mushrooms, finely chopped
14 oz can chopped tomatoes
4 teaspoons tomato paste
1 small carrot, grated
1 small zucchini, diced
4 teaspoons vegetable bouillon
14 oz can brown lentils, rinsed and
    drained
½ cup cooked brown rice
¼ cup chopped flat-leaf (Italian)
    parsley

POTATO TOPPING

3 large all-purpose potatoes, diced
½ teaspoon sea salt
2½ tablespoons oat milk
4 teaspoons olive oil
pinch paprika

Grease a 9 inch round pie dish, about 1½ inches deep.

To make the spelt pastry, sift both of the flours and salt together into a large bowl. Using your fingers, rub the oil into the flour until the mixture resembles fine breadcrumbs. Gradually stir in ⅓ cup boiling water until the mixture forms a dough. Turn out onto a lightly floured surface and knead the dough gently until smooth. Roll the pastry between two sheets of parchment paper to a circle about ⅛ inch thick. Carefully lower the pastry into the dish to line, trimming any excess. Set aside.

To make the lentil filling, heat the oil in a large saucepan over medium–high heat. Add the onion, garlic and pepper and cook for about 5 minutes, stirring often, until the onion softens. Add the mushrooms and cook for 5 minutes, or until softened. Add the tomatoes, tomato paste and ¾ cup water. Bring to a boil. Add the carrot, zucchini, bouillon, lentils and rice. Reduce the heat to medium–low and simmer, uncovered, for 10 minutes, or until the vegetables are tender and the mixture has thickened. Stir in the parsley and set aside to cool.

Preheat the oven to 400°F.

To make the potato topping, cook the potatoes in a large saucepan of boiling water for 15 minutes, or until very tender. Drain well and mash together with the salt, oat milk and oil until well combined and smooth.

Spoon the cooled lentil filling over the pastry in the dish and layer the mashed potato over the top. Sprinkle with the paprika and bake for about 40 minutes, or until the topping is lightly browned. Remove from the oven and allow to stand for 10 minutes before cutting into slices and serving.

ocean trout with cauliflower purée and lime balsamic dressing

serves 4

4 x 6 oz skinless ocean trout fillets

¾ cup freshly squeezed orange juice

⅓ cup chopped dill

1 small cauliflower, cut into small florets

½ cup macadamia oil

4 baby bok choy heads, trimmed and halved, to serve

LIME BALSAMIC DRESSING

3½ tablespoons macadamia oil

3½ tablespoons freshly squeezed lime juice

2½ tablespoons white balsamic vinegar

1 teaspoon Dijon mustard

Put the trout, orange juice and dill in a glass or ceramic dish and turn the fillets to coat in the marinade. Cover with plastic wrap and refrigerate for 3 hours.

To make the lime balsamic dressing, put the macadamia oil, lime juice, vinegar and mustard in a small bowl and whisk well until combined. Set aside until needed.

Preheat the oven to 400°F. Line a baking sheet with parchment paper.

Cook the cauliflower in a large saucepan of boiling water for 15–20 minutes, or until very tender. Drain well, then transfer to a food processor with all but 1 tablespoon of the macadamia oil and process until smooth. Cover to keep warm.

Remove the fillets from the marinade and pat dry with paper towel. Heat the remaining macadamia oil in a large frying pan and cook the trout for 4 minutes on each side, or until browned. Transfer to the prepared sheet and bake for 8–10 minutes, or until cooked to your liking.

Meanwhile, bring a large saucepan of water to a boil. Add the bok choy and blanch for 30 seconds, or until tender. Drain well.

Divide the cauliflower purée between serving plates, top with the trout and drizzle the lime balsamic dressing over the top. Serve with the blanched bok choy alongside.

bean and potato tacos
makes 10

2 large all-purpose potatoes,
  diced
4 teaspoons olive oil
14 oz can red kidney beans,
  rinsed and drained
freshly squeezed juice of ½ lemon
10 taco shells
¼ small iceberg lettuce,
  shredded, to serve
3 ripe plum tomatoes, diced,
  to serve
1 carrot, grated, to serve
1 small avocado, peeled, stone
  removed and flesh diced, to
  serve
½ green pepper, seeded,
  membrane removed and
  diced, to serve
1 small handful sunflower sprouts,
  to serve

TACO SEASONING
1 teaspoon cayenne pepper
½ teaspoon garlic powder
½ teaspoon onion powder
4 teaspoons ground cumin
½ teaspoon dry mustard
1 teaspoon sea salt
1 teaspoon paprika
½ teaspoon ground coriander

To make the taco seasoning combine all the ingredients in a small bowl and stir to combine. Store in an airtight container until needed.

Preheat the oven to 400°F.

Cook the potatoes in a saucepan of boiling water for about 10 minutes, or until just tender. Drain well, then transfer to a baking sheet, drizzle over the olive oil and sprinkle over half of the taco seasoning. Bake in the oven for 20 minutes, or until golden.

Put the beans, lemon juice and remaining taco seasoning into a small saucepan over medium heat and cook for about 5 minutes, stirring often, until warmed through.

Heat the taco shells according to the package directions. To serve, fill each taco shell with some beans, potato, lettuce, tomato, carrot, avocado, pepper and sprouts.

peppers with tomato bean filling

serves 4

2½ tablespoons olive oil

1 yellow onion, finely chopped

2 garlic cloves, crushed

½ small eggplant, finely diced

4 oz button mushrooms, finely chopped

¼ cup flat-leaf (Italian) parsley, finely chopped

4 teaspoons finely chopped oregano

4 ripe plum tomatoes, chopped

14 oz can borlotti beans, rinsed and drained

¼ cup stale breadcrumbs

¼ cup finely grated parmesan cheese or vegan parmesan cheese (see page 76)

4 large red peppers, seeded, membrane removed and halved lengthwise, leaving the stalks attached

Heat 1 tablespoon of the oil in a large frying pan over medium–high heat. Add the onion and garlic and cook for about 5 minutes, stirring often, until the onion softens. Add the eggplant, mushrooms, parsley, oregano and tomatoes. Cook for about 5 minutes, stirring regularly until the eggplant is cooked. Remove from the heat and transfer to a large bowl. Set aside to cool slightly.

Preheat the oven to 350°F.

Add the beans, breadcrumbs and cheese to the eggplant mixture and stir well to combine.

Brush the peppers on the skin side with the remaining olive oil. Place the pepper halves, cut side up, in a baking dish. Divide the bean mixture between the pepper halves and bake for 45 minutes, or until the pepper is tender and the filling is golden. Serve the filled pepper with your favorite salad and dressing (see pages 80–107).

balinese chicken curry
serves 4

4 teaspoons coconut oil (see note
   page 36)

2 cups coconut milk

4 teaspoons grated palm sugar
   (jaggery)

2½ tablespoons fish sauce

1 kaffir lime leaf

1¼ lbs chicken breast fillets,
   thinly sliced

steamed jasmine rice, to serve

CURRY PASTE

3 yellow onions, coarsely chopped

4 garlic cloves, halved

8 long red chiles, seeded and
   chopped

1¼ inch piece fresh ginger,
   chopped

¼ cup chopped pickled galangal
   or 1¼ inch piece fresh galangal,
   chopped (see note)

2½ tablespoons grated fresh
   turmeric

2½ tablespoons finely chopped
   cilantro root and stem

1 lemongrass stem, white part
   only, thinly sliced

To make the curry paste, put all of the ingredients into a food processor and process until well combined. Set aside until needed.

Heat the coconut oil in a large saucepan over medium–high heat. Scoop the coconut cream from the top of the coconut milk and add to the pan, stirring, until the oil separates from the coconut. Add the palm sugar, fish sauce and 1 cup of the curry paste and stir for 1 minute, or until aromatic. Add the coconut milk and lime leaf and bring just to the boil. Reduce the heat to medium–low and simmer, uncovered, for 10 minutes. Add the chicken and cook for 5 minutes, or until cooked through and the sauce has reduced. Serve with the steamed jasmine rice.

Note: Any leftover curry paste can be stored in an airtight container in the refrigerator for up to 4 days, or frozen for up to 3 months.

Galangal can be subsituted with pickled or fresh ginger.

lentil and squash loaf
serves 8

1 cup brown lentils, rinsed

¾ lb butternut squash, peeled, seeded and cut into ½ inch pieces

2 yellow onions, finely chopped

3 cups fresh breadcrumbs

2½ tablespoons finely chopped flat-leaf (Italian) parsley

4 teaspoons finely chopped thyme

½ cup whole milk

Preheat the oven to 375°F. Lightly grease an 8 x 4 x 2 ½ inch loaf pan.

Put the lentils into a saucepan, cover with water and bring to a boil over high heat. Reduce the heat and simmer for 20 minutes, or until tender. Rinse the cooked lentils under cold running water, drain well, transfer to a large bowl and set aside.

Meanwhile, cook the squash in a large saucepan of boiling water for 10 minutes, or until tender. Drain and set aside.

Mash the lentils, then add the squash, onion, breadcrumbs, parsley and thyme and stir well to combine. Gradually add the milk and continue stirring until the mixture just comes together.

Spoon the mixture into the prepared pan. Using the back of the spoon, press the mixture firmly into the prepared pan. Bake in the oven for 30 minutes, or until the loaf is firm to the touch. Remove from the oven and allow to cool in the pan for 10 minutes before turning out and slicing into thick slices. Serve immediately.

Tip: You can sprinkle 1 tablespoon toasted sesame seeds over the base and sides of the prepared pan before adding the lentil mixture and baking.

chicken with ginger and orange stuffing
serves 4

⅔ cup fresh gluten-free
  breadcrumbs
finely grated zest of ½ orange
½ teaspoon finely grated fresh
  ginger
1 scallion, thinly sliced
½ kaffir lime leaf, finely chopped
½ garlic clove, crushed
2 teaspoons finely chopped
  cilantro leaves
1 free-range egg yolk, lightly
  beaten
4 x 6 oz chicken breast fillets
4 teaspoons olive oil
steamed baby carrots, to serve
quinoa salad (see page 81), to
  serve

Preheat the oven to 400°F. Line a baking sheet with parchment paper.

Put the breadcrumbs, orange zest, ginger, scallion, lime leaf, garlic, cilantro and egg yolk in a bowl and mix well to combine.

Use a small sharp knife to cut a horizontal slit in the thickest part of each chicken breast to create a pocket. Divide the breadcrumb mixture into four even-sized portions and spoon into each pocket.

Heat the oil in a large frying pan over high heat. Cook the chicken for 2–3 minutes on each side, or until browned. Transfer the chicken to the prepared sheet and bake for 15 minutes, or until the chicken is cooked through.

Serve the chicken breasts with the steamed carrots and quinoa salad on the side.

tamarind glazed salmon with wasabi yogurt

serves 2

½ small orange sweet potato

½ small daikon radish

2½ tablespoons tamarind purée (see note)

4 teaspoons mirin

4 teaspoons grated palm sugar (jaggery)

pinch sea salt

1 teaspoon sunflower oil or light olive oil

2 x 6 oz salmon fillets, skin on

¼ cup plain yogurt

½ teaspoon wasabi paste

2½ tablespoons soy sauce

2 bok choy heads, trimmed and halved

Preheat the oven to 350°F. Line a baking sheet with parchment paper.

Peel and cut the sweet potato into batons, each about 2 x ½ inches thick (try to make them as even as possible, as it adds a slight sense of formality to this dish). Repeat with the radish. Steam the potato and radish for about 12 minutes, or until tender.

Combine the tamarind, mirin, palm sugar, salt and oil in a small bowl. Place the salmon on the prepared sheet and spread a heaping teaspoon of the tamarind mixture over each salmon fillet (leftover tamarind mixture will keep, covered, in the refrigerator for up to 1 week). Bake for 8–10 minutes, or until cooked through.

Meanwhile combine the yogurt and wasabi in a small bowl.

Put the soy sauce and ¼ cup water in a frying pan and bring to a boil. Add the bok choy and cook for 2–4 minutes, turning occasionally, or until just tender.

Arrange the sweet potato and radish batons with the bok choy on serving plates and top with the salmon fillets. Spoon a little wasabi yogurt over the salmon and serve immediately.

Note: Tamarind purée, also known as tamarind concentrate, is available in jars from the Asian section of selected supermarkets and from Asian grocery stores. It is an essential ingredient in many Asian dishes and adds a distinct tartness.

This dish is contemporary Japanese in its style, it is simple to prepare, looks beautiful on the plate, and is a very delicious and healthy meal. In this dish the salmon is cooked through, and not left rare in the middle — it is a Gaia favorite.

falafels

serves 4

1 small yellow onion, chopped

2 garlic cloves, chopped

¼ cup flat-leaf (Italian) parsley

freshly squeezed juice of 1 lemon

¼ cup olive oil

1 cup sprouted chickpeas (see
    page 14)

½ cup sesame seeds, soaked in
    water for 1 hour, then drained

1 cup almonds, soaked in water
    for 1 hour, then drained

1 cup walnuts, soaked in water
    for 1 hour, then drained

¼ teaspoon cayenne pepper

1 teaspoon sea salt

1½ teaspoons ground cumin

1½ teaspoons ground coriander

sprouted hummus dip (see
    page 75), to serve

tabouleh and avocado salad (see
    page 93), to serve

Preheat the oven to 350°F. Line a baking sheet with parchment paper.

Put the onion, garlic, parsley, lemon juice and oil into a food processor and process until well combined. Add the remaining ingredients but not the hummus dip and tabbouleh and ¼ cup water and process until well combined and the mixture comes together to form a thick paste — you may need to add a little extra water if the mixture is too dry.

Take heaping tablespoons of the mixture at a time and roll into neat balls. Repeat to make about 30 falafels in total. Place on the prepared sheet and bake for 25 minutes, turning once during cooking, or until lightly browned and firm to the touch.

Serve the falafels with the sprouted hummus dip and the tabouleh and avocado salad on the side.

sweets

cashew, macadamia and raspberry tart

serves 8–10

¼ cup shredded coconut

2 cups macadamia nuts

½ cup pitted dried dates, chopped

FILLING

2 cups cashews, soaked in water overnight, then drained

freshly squeezed juice of 1 lemon

¼ cup agave syrup (see note page 22)

¼ cup coconut oil (see note page 36), warmed

1 teaspoon natural vanilla extract

RASPBERRY TOPPING

2 cups thawed frozen or fresh raspberries

½ cup pitted dried dates, chopped

Lightly grease a round 8½ inch spring-form cake pan. Line the base with parchment paper and dust with the coconut.

Put the macadamias and dates into a food processor and process until well combined. Press the date mixture over the coconut in the base of the pan.

To make the filling, put the cashews, lemon juice, agave syrup, coconut oil, vanilla extract and ½ cup water into a food processor and process until well combined and smooth. Pour over the date mixture in the pan. Lightly tap the pan on a work surface to remove any air bubbles. Cover with plastic wrap and freeze for at least 2 hours, or until the filling is firm.

To make the topping, put the raspberries and dates in a food processor and process until smooth.

Remove the tart from the pan and transfer to a serving plate. Top with the raspberry topping and serve in wedges.

mulled pears with toasted muesli

serves 6

2 cups red wine

½ cup sugar, plus extra, to taste

¼ cup honey

finely grated zest of 1 lemon

finely grated zest of 1 lime

1 cinnamon stick

3 cloves

2 star anise

1 mint sprig

1¼ cup water

6 pears, peeled, halved and cored
   with stems attached

plain yogurt, to serve

MUESLI

1 cup rolled oats

½ cup shredded coconut

⅓ cup pumpkin seeds

2 oz sunflower seeds

2 oz sliced almonds

⅓ cup sesame seeds

pinch ground cinnamon

pinch freshly grated nutmeg

Put the wine, sugar, honey, citrus zests, spices and mint into a saucepan with 1¼ cups of water. Bring to a boil, then reduce the heat and simmer for 5 minutes. Add the halved pears and continue to simmer for about 45 minutes, or until the pears are tender but still holding their shape (the time will vary depending on the ripeness of the pears). Remove from the heat and leave the pears to cool in the syrup.

Preheat the oven to 400°F. Combine all of the muesli ingredients and spread them in an even layer on a baking sheet. Cook for 6–8 minutes, or until lightly toasted.

Drain the pears and set aside. Return the cooking syrup to high heat and add the extra sugar, to taste. Bring to a boil and cook for about 5 minutes, or until it thickens. Remove from the heat and cool.

Serve the pears with a little syrup spooned over and each half sprinkled with about 1 tablespoon of the muesli. Top with a dollop of yogurt.

Note: Any leftover muesli will keep in an airtight container for up to 2 weeks.

pear and oatmeal yogurt muffins
makes 18

olive oil spray, for greasing
2 cups all-purpose flour
1 tablespoon baking powder
½ teaspoon baking soda
1 teaspoon pumpkin pie spice or
    ground cinnamon
⅔ cup rolled oats
½ cup superfine sugar
2 ripe pears or apples, cored and
    diced with skin on
2 free-range eggs, lightly beaten
1½ cups mixed berry or
    strawberry yogurt
½ cup vegetable oil

Preheat the oven to 350°F. Lightly grease a 12-hole standard ½ cup capacity muffin tin with olive oil spray.

Sift the flour, baking powder, baking soda and pumpkin pie spice into a large bowl. Stir in the oats, sugar and pear.

In a separate bowl, put the egg, yogurt and vegetable oil and stir well to combine. Add to the dry ingredients and stir until just combined.

Divide the mixture evenly between the muffin holes and bake for 15–20 minutes, or until a knife inserted into the middle of the muffins comes out clean. Remove from the oven and turn out onto a wire rack to cool slightly. Serve warm or at room temperature.

Livvy's easy baked apples

serves 4

4 apples or pears, cored

⅓ cup dried fruit, such as raisins
   or cranberries

1 cup freshly squeezed orange
   juice

2½ tablespoons honey or maple
   syrup

plain yogurt or ice cream,
   to serve (optional)

Preheat the oven to 350°F.

Use a sharp knife to make a shallow cut through the skin around the middle of the apple — this prevents the skin from splitting during cooking.

Place the dried fruit into the cavity of the apples and arrange the apples in a small baking dish. Pour over the orange juice and drizzle over the honey. Bake the apples for about 30 minutes, or until the juice has thickened and the apples are soft. Remove from the oven and serve warm with yogurt or ice cream, if desired.

I use pears for this too! It's a favorite in our house and it's an easy healthy fix for our "sweet tooth." Chloe loved this as a little girl!

summer pudding

serves 6

8 slices bread, crusts removed,
  or panettone
3 cups fresh or thawed frozen
  mixed berries
½ cup superfine sugar
vanilla yogurt, to serve

Line a 4 cup capacity dessert mold with the bread slices, cutting them to fit the mold exactly, with a slight overlap.

Put the berries and sugar into a saucepan over medium heat. Cook very gently for 5 minutes, or until the fruit is tender. Drain the berries, reserving ½ cup of the cooking juice.

Spoon the berries over the bread in the mold, packing it in well. Pour in the reserved juice. Arrange the remaining bread on top of the fruit in an even layer. Cover with a plate, small enough to rest on the pudding, then place a pan or other weight over the plate to weigh it down. Refrigerate overnight.

To serve, turn the pudding out of the mold and serve with vanilla yogurt.

easy blueberry yogurt and muesli parfait
serves 4–6

1⅔ cups blueberries

3⅓ cups strawberries, hulled and sliced

2 cups natural muesli (see page 26)

14 oz blueberry yogurt

¼ cup sliced almonds, toasted

Scatter half of the combined blueberries and strawberries in the base of four serving glasses. Top with a layer of muesli, then a generous dollop of yogurt. Repeat with another layer of fruit, muesli and yogurt, then garnish with any leftover berries and the sliced almonds.

Make this parfait when summer berries are at their peak.

panforte bars
makes about 24 pieces

7 oz dark chocolate, melted

1½ cups blanched almonds, toasted

1½ cups pistachio nuts

½ cup finely chopped candied citrus peel

6 oz chopped dried apricots, golden raisins or figs

1½ cups honey, warmed

1 cup all-purpose flour or rice flour, sifted

2½ tablespoons raw cacao powder, sifted (see note)

½ teaspoon pumpkin pie spice

1 teaspoon ground cinnamon

Preheat the oven to 325°F. Line a 11 x 7 inch baking pan with parchment paper.

Put the chocolate, nuts, citrus peel and dried apricots in a large bowl. Stir in the warm honey until well combined.

Combine the flour, cacao powder, pumpkin pie spice and cinnamon in a separate bowl then fold through the chocolate mixture until well combined. Spread the mixture into the prepared pan and bake for 45 minutes, or until just set — the bars should be slightly moist, similar to brownies.

Remove from the oven and allow to cool completely in the pan before cutting into bars and serving.

Note: Cacao powder is similar to cocoa powder but is less refined and has a greater nutritional content. You can find it at health food stores or online. Cocoa powder can be substituted if you can't find cacao powder.

John and I love anything chocolate — and it's good for you! This is like a fancy brownie!

oatmeal cookies
makes 25

2 cups rolled oats

1 cup shredded coconut

6 oz pitted dried dates, chopped

1 cup ricotta cheese

⅓ cup golden syrup (see note)

3 free-range eggs

¼ cup cold-pressed oil of your
choice

2 large ripe bananas, mashed

Preheat the oven to 350°F. Line a baking sheet with parchment paper.

Combine the oats, coconut and dates in a large bowl.

In a separate bowl, beat together the ricotta cheese, golden syrup, eggs, oil and mashed banana until well combined. Add to the dry ingredients and stir well until the mixture holds together — if it is crumbly, add a little water, a small amount at a time, stirring well after each addition.

Drop 1 tablespoonful of the mixture at a time onto the prepared sheet, leaving enough room for spreading between each one. Use a fork to flatten the mixture slightly. Bake for about 20 minutes, or until cooked through. Remove from the oven and allow to cool on the tray for 10 minutes, before transferring to a wire rack to cool completely.

The oatmeal cookies can be stored in an airtight container for up to 10 days.

Tip: Instead of dates, you can use the same quantity of drained soaked raisins, golden raisins or chopped dried apricots. If you like, sprinkle some sesame seeds over the top of each cookie before baking.

Note: Golden syrup is a clear golden liquid sweetener with the consistency of corn syrup. Popular in Australia and the UK, it can be found in selected supermarkets and gourmet markets. A combination of two parts light corn syrup and one part molasses can be substituted.

Oh so good with my cup of tea after a strong workout!

date and walnut truffles

makes 15–20

2 cups walnuts

1 cup pitted dried dates

4 teaspoons coconut oil (see note page 36)

¼ cup carob powder

¼ cup shredded coconut

Put all of the ingredients except the coconut into a food processor and process until smooth.

Take 1 teaspoon of mixture at a time and roll it into a neat ball. Roll each truffle in coconut to evenly coat all over. Refrigerate until ready to serve.

Note: These truffles will keep in an airtight container in the refrigerator for up to 2 weeks. Serve at room temperature.

So tasty! I like the real thing yet you can use cacao instead of carob if you prefer.

mango tart with date and macadamia crust

serves 8

2½ tablespoons ground almonds
1¼ cups pitted dried dates
¾ cup macadamia nuts
2 teaspoons agar agar powder
   (see note)
2 large ripe mangoes

Lightly grease a round 8 inch spring-form cake pan. Dust the base with the ground almonds.

Place the dates in an ovenproof bowl and pour over enough boiling water to cover. Stand for 20 minutes. Drain well and coarsely chop the dates.

Put the dates and macadamia nuts in a food processor and process until well combined. Press the date mixture in an even layer into the base of the pan.

Put ½ cup water in a small saucepan and add the agar agar. Set aside for 5 minutes to soak. Bring to a boil over high heat, stirring. Reduce the heat and simmer gently for 3–4 minutes or until the agar agar is completely dissolved. Remove from the heat.

Peel the mangoes, remove the stones, roughly chop the flesh and place it in a blender and blend until smooth. Add the mango purée to the agar agar mixture, stirring constantly until evenly combined. Working quickly, pour the mango mixture into the pan. Cover with plastic wrap and refrigerate for at least 2 hours, or until set. Transfer to a serving plate, cut into slices and serve.

The mango tart can be stored, covered, in the refrigerator for up to 3 days.

Note: Agar agar is a natural gelling agent made from seaweed and can be used instead of gelatin. It only dissolves in boiling water. It is available from health food stores.

orange, almond and polenta cake

serves 10–12

2 lb oranges, scrubbed

9 free-range eggs

2 cups ground almonds

6 oz polenta

10½ oz xylitol (see note page 33)

1 tablespoon baking powder

¼ cup sliced almonds

Put the oranges into a large saucepan and cover with water. Bring to a boil over medium heat and cook the oranges, changing the water every 30 minutes or so, for 3 hours, or until the oranges are very tender (changing the water reduces the bitterness of the peel). Refresh the oranges under cold running water and drain well. Coarsely chop the oranges, discarding any seeds and the cores.

Preheat the oven to 350°F. Line the base of a round 9 inch spring-form cake pan with parchment paper.

Put the orange flesh in a food processor and process until finely chopped. Add the eggs and process until well combined. Transfer to a large bowl and stir in the ground almonds, polenta, xylitol and baking powder until combined.

Pour the mixture into the prepared pan and sprinkle the sliced almonds over the top. Bake for 1 hour–1 hour 30 minutes, or until a knife inserted into the center of the cake comes out clean. Remove from the oven and allow to cool in the pan for 15 minutes before transferring to a wire rack to cool completely.

blueberry muffins
makes 12

olive oil spray, for greasing
1 cup fresh or frozen blueberries
4 teaspoons soft brown sugar
2 cups whole wheat self-rising
   flour
1 teaspoon baking powder
1 teaspoon ground cinnamon
1 free-range egg, beaten
½ cup low-fat berry yogurt
1 cup low-fat milk

Preheat the oven to 425°F. Lightly grease a 12-hole standard ½ cup muffin tin with olive oil spray or line with baking cups.

Put the blueberries and sugar in a saucepan over medium heat. Stir until the juices just start to run and the sugar dissolves. Remove from the heat and set aside to cool.

Sift the flour, baking powder and cinnamon into a bowl.

In a separate bowl, combine the egg, yogurt and milk. Add to the dry ingredients and stir until well combined. Gently fold in the cooled blueberry mixture until combined.

Spoon the mixture evenly between the muffin holes and bake for 15–20 minutes, or until a knife inserted into the center of the muffins comes out clean. Remove from the oven and turn out onto a wire rack to cool.

Sometimes I use raspberries or cranberries for a change.

author biographies

Olivia Newton-John

Born in Cambridge, England, in 1948, the youngest child of Professor Brin Newton-John and Irene, daughter of Nobel Prize-winning physicist, Max Born, Olivia moved to Melbourne, Australia, with her family when she was five. By the age of fifteen, she had formed an all-girl group called Sol Four. Later that year she won a talent contest on the popular TV show, *Sing, Sing, Sing*, which earned her a trip to London. By 1963, Olivia was appearing on local daytime TV shows and weekly pop music programs in Australia. Olivia cut her first single for Decca Records in 1966, a version of Jackie DeShannon's "Till You Say You'll Be Mine."

Olivia's US album debut, *Let Me Be There*, produced her first top-ten single of the same name, with Olivia being honored by the Academy of Country Music as Most Promising Female Vocalist and a Grammy Award as Best Country Vocalist. This proved to be only the beginning of a very exciting career. With more than 100 million albums sold, her successes include three more Grammys, numerous Country Music, American Music, and People's Choice Awards, ten number-one hits including "Physical," which topped the charts for ten consecutive weeks, and over 15 top-ten singles. In 1978, her co-starring role with John Travolta in *Grease* catapulted Olivia into super-stardom. To date *Grease* remains the most successful movie musical in history. Her other film credits include *Xanadu*, *Two of a Kind*, *It's My Party* and *Sordid Lives*. Her latest film, *A Few Best Men,* will be released in January 2012.

Olivia's appeal seems to be timeless. With a career spanning more than four decades she is still a vibrant, creative individual who is adored by fans across the world. Throughout her career, the much-loved star was bestowed an O.B.E. (Order of the British Empire) by Queen Elizabeth in 1979 and has held many humanitarian causes close to her heart, particularly since the birth of her daughter, Chloe, in 1986. Olivia served as Goodwill Ambassador to the United Nations Environment Programme and in 1991, the Colette Chuda Environmental Fund/CHEC (Children's Health Environmental Coalition) was founded after the tragic death of Chloe's best friend from a rare childhood cancer, with Olivia serving as National Spokesperson for ten years. (For more information visit www.healthychild.org.)

Her charmed life has not been without its share of upset. In the 90s, Olivia successfully overcame her own battle with breast cancer, which inspired her album, *GAIA*, her most personal album reflecting upon her experiences with cancer. She used these experiences to gain greater self-awareness and became a positive inspiration to millions of people battling cancer. Her personal victory against cancer led her to announce her partnership with Austin Health and the creation of the Olivia Newton-John Cancer and Wellness Centre (ONJCWC) on the Austin Campus in her hometown of Melbourne, Australia (www.oliviaappeal.com).

Continuing her efforts to find a cure for breast cancer, Olivia launched Liv Aid®, a breast self-examination aid that assists women to administer breast self-exams correctly (www.liv.com).

In 1999, Olivia garnered an Emmy Award for her songwriting and returned to work as a performer touring extensively in the United States for the first time in seventeen years. In 2002, Olivia was inducted into the prestigious Australian Music Hall of Fame at the 16th Annual Aria Awards. Then, in 2006, she received the Lifetime Achievement Award, presented by friend John Travolta at the G'Day L.A. Gala. Her passion for Australia was proven once again when Olivia reunited with friend and business partner Pat Farrar to launch their distinctly Australian wines under the iconic homegrown brand Koala Blue, to proudly bring the "Taste of Australia" to the rest of the world. In February 2005, along with her business partners Gregg Cave, Warwick Evans and Ruth Kalnin, Olivia opened the Gaia Retreat & Spa in Byron Bay, New South Wales, Australia, as an ideal place to renew, refresh and restore.

In 2008 Olivia married Amazon Herb Company owner and founder, John "Amazon John" Easterling (www.amazonherb.com). Together Olivia and John are spreading the word about the importance of preserving the rainforest and the health values found in the botanicals of the Amazon. In addition, they are working together with the ACEER Organization (www.aceer.org) to help the indigenous people of the Amazon gain ownership and title to their land. In September 2009, they also joined forces with Prince Charles's The Prince's Rainforest Project (www.rainforestsos.org) to further stress the global importance of the rainforest. With the release of the Amazon Herb Company skin care system, Amazon Rain, Olivia continues to spread the word about rainforest botanicals while at the same time reveals the product as the secret behind her radiant skin (www.amazonrain.com).

For additional information visit www.olivianewton-john.com or follow her on Twitter @OliviaNJ or become a fan on Facebook at www.facebook.com/olivianewtonjohn.

author biographies

Kristine S. Matheson

Kristine S. Matheson was born in Sydney and is the author of the bestselling book *From Cancer to Wellness: The Forgotten Secrets*. In 2005, Kristine was diagnosed with stage IV melanoma cancer and given only twelve months to live. Instead of accepting this as her fate, and with her knowledge of nutrition, strong determination, together with a positive attitude, she overcame all obstacles. Kristine became cancer-free within a few short months without any medical intervention. Kristine is passionate about treating the cause of disease and now works with her husband, Wayne Matheson, regularly holding Wellness Seminars, Cancer Support Groups plus Weight Loss Challenges for charity, incorporating her healthy food knowledge with Wayne's safe personal training techniques to benefit those in her community on the Gold Coast, Australia. She has been nominated for the "Who's Who of Australian Women" award 2011–2012 and was the recipient of the International Women's Day 2011, "Outstanding Inspirational Role Model" award. For more information about Kristine Matheson go to www.cancertowellness.com or www.theforgottensecrets.com.

Karen Inge APD FSMA FSDA

Karen Inge is one of Australia's best-known accredited practicing dietitians. She is the nutrition writer for the *Australian Women's Weekly* and regularly comments and makes appearances on radio and TV current affairs programs. She is also known for her high-profile career as a sports dietitian, working with elite athletes and developing nutrition programs for sporting organizations, as well as global food companies. An award-winning author, Karen is a sought-after speaker for her inspiring presentations to the medical and dietetic professions, as well as the corporate, education and sporting communities. She holds board positions with Jenny Craig and the Coeliac Research Fund. For more information about Karen Inge go to www.kareninge.com.

Dereck Cooper

Dereck Cooper is head chef at Gaia Retreat and Spa in Byron Bay, Australia. After taking a five-year sabbatical from his career as a chef, Dereck decided to work in the neurological field and learned a lot about the amazing benefits food can have on mind, body and soul. Returning to the kitchen with renewed enthusiasm, Dereck now embraces a holistic approach to cooking—using food as a medicine.

Leah Roland

Founding Principal of the Bangalow Cooking School, Leah has also run a catering business in Sydney and published many food articles in Australia. She has implemented a health and lifestyle cooking program at The Buttery, a leading drug and alcohol rehabilitation facility in Binna Burra, NSW, and placed educational food programs in many regional schools. Leah has now joined the Gaia team as a chef where she relishes the holistic approach to fundamentally good food.

Campbell Rowe

Born and raised on an olive orchard in the Wairarapa, New Zealand, Campbell moved to Australia after completing his chef training in 1999. Taking a position at Yandina's Spirit House restaurant on the Sunshine Coast, he developed a love for Thai and Asian-inspired cuisine. He eventually moved to the Byron Shire to study organic farming in production horticulture at Wollongbar Primary Industries Institute. After qualifying in 2008, he took a traineeship on an organic farm to help establish a 6,000-hen free-range egg operation. He is currently employed as Gaia's sous chef and enjoys working with fresh produce from the organic garden.

Toni Golds

Toni has been working at Gaia Retreat and Spa for three years. She is also studying at the Wollongbar TAFE Northern Rivers NSW.

index

First published in 2011 by Murdoch Books Pty Limited
First Lyons Press edition, 2012

Lyons Press is an imprint of Globe Pequot Press
Library of Congress Cataloguing-in-Publication Data is available on file

Photographer (Food): Natasha Milne
Photographer (Olivia and cover): Michele Aboud
Stylist: Jody Vassallo
Project Manager: Livia Caiazzo
Editor: Jacqueline Blanchard
Designer: Tania Gomes
Production Controller: Joan Beal

IMPORTANT: Those who are most vulnerable to salmonella poisoning (the elderly, pregnant women, young children and those suffering from immune deficiency diseases) should consult their doctor with any concerns about eating raw eggs.

OVEN GUIDE: You may find cooking times vary depending on the oven you are using. For convection ovens, as a general rule, set the oven temperature to 35°F lower than indicated in the recipe.

RECIPE CONTRIBUTORS:
Kristine Matheson: pages 25, 26, 30, 33, 34, 35, 36, 45, 50, 52, 53, 54, 59, 60, 64, 70, 71 (bottom), 72, 75, 76, 77, 82, 89 (bottom), 91, 98, 102, 120, 123, 129, 130, 134, 141, 150, 151 (top),164, 176, 180.
Toni Golds: pages 22, 29, 39, 81, 115
Todd Cameron: pages 159, 179
Campbell Rowe: page 85
Michael Jennings: page 90
Leah Roland: pages 93, 94, 102 (bottom), 105 (top), 160, 172
Dereck Cooper: pages 68, 71 (top), 111, 112, 124, 142, 152, 156
Karen Inge: pages 27, 40, 41, 52 (bottom), 85 (top), 107 (top), 118, 119, 126, 127, 155, 166, 167, 170, 171, 175

ISBN 978-0-7627-8009-9

PRINTED IN CHINA

10 9 8 7 6 5 4 3 2 1